A RANT OF RAVENS
A Bird Watchers Mystery

Chris Goff

© Christ Goff 2000

Chris Goff has asserted her rights under the Copyright, Design and Patents Act, 1988, to be identified as the author of this work.

First published 2000 by Berkley.

This edition published in 2020 by Sharpe Books.

For Maggie Osborne, my friend and mentor.
Thanks for pushing me down the path.

CONTENTS

Introduction
Chapters 1 – 18
Common Raven
Acknowledgements

Introduction

When I first started writing A Rant of Ravens, I had a lot to learn about birding. As a backyard birdwatcher, I'd rarely birded in the field, yet I knew the environment was where the stories existed. Hence, I needed a setting. Writers often are told: write what you know. The idea behind this is that you have less to research and familiarity lends authenticity to the work. Raised in Colorado, near the gateway to one of the world's birding hot spots—Rocky Mountain National Park—it stands to reason I set my book in Estes Park—oops Elk Lake. (The publisher insisted on a fictional town.) And I was familiar with many of the birds.

Next, I needed a crime. I remember a park ranger I knew telling a story about a peregrine eyas (youngster) being stolen from a nest in the park and delivered to a sheikh in Saudi Arabia for $100K. Peregrines are commonly used for hunting in the Middle East and often bred in captivity, and the sheikh felt the program-bred birds had lost their instinctual edge. The young eyas would provide an infusion of wild blood. In this case, the culprits were caught, justice was meted out, and it provided a kernel from which my story grew.

I also needed some hands-on field-birding experience. The year was 1998, the 5th Annual Rio Grande Valley Birding Festival was being held in Harlingen, Texas, and I signed up for a crash course in birding. Thinking a canoe trip on the Rio Grande sounded fun, I soon found myself mid-river, in a tippy boat, with one of sixteen world-class birders. Lesson #1, I needed a better pair of binoculars, and I'd been using the ones I had incorrectly, for years. Still, we witnessed baptisms taking place in the water on the Mexican side, discovered fossils, and spotted birds—lots of birds. For me, many were life birds (those I'd never seen before). A few target-birds remained elusive, but—experienced birders or novice—we developed a camaraderie through shared adventure.

After observing the thousands of visitors to the Birders Bazaar Trade Show and the 600+ taking part in the field trips, I came away from Harlingen knowing I needed one more thing—characters. I needed to create protagonists who had a commitment to promoting the welfare of birds and their environment and a vested interest in solving the mystery.

In A Rant of Ravens, that character is Rachel Wilder Stanhope. She's a non-birdwatcher, a fast-tracker from NYC, who comes to Elk Park to visit her Aunt Miriam. Pressed into various birding activities, such as pishing for birds (check out the book), she stumbles upon the body of a reporter who was in town to nose around an old story. But while Rachel is busy sorting out possible motives, three rare birds go missing—and Miriam disappears without a trace...

Chapter 1

Dipped out?

"What, exactly, does that mean, Aunt Miriam?" Rachel Stanhope shouldered the telephone receiver and rooted in the overstuffed filing cabinet for the Henderson design folder. The pendulum clock ticked toward the Monday morning production meeting, signaling a need to end the conversation, but curiosity had gotten the better of her. "An abbreviated version."

"It's an expression I picked up birdwatching in the British Isles. Specifically, as defined by Peter Weaver in The Birdwatcher's Dictionary, it means 'failing to see a rare bird which other birdwatchers have succeeded in seeing.' In your case, dear, it means you viewed Roger as a bald eagle while the rest of us spotted a turkey."

"Aunt Miriam, I can honestly say I've never once thought of Roger as a bird." Unlike her aunt, who classified everything in bird terms, Rachel viewed the world from a more nonsectarian perspective. "Try a larger species."

"Canine?"

"I was thinking equine." Two months ago, Rachel had come home from work and found her husband in bed with a waitress from the West Side Diner. Roger, ranked seventeenth on the PGA tour, had called it a bogey, cited the "seven-year itch," and taken a penalty stroke.

"Well, if you ask me," said Miriam, "the man's a dodo."

Rachel swallowed against the sudden, rising lump in her throat. Aunt Miriam had always been her biggest cheerleader. More importantly, she stuck like ink to paper whenever the chips were down. "I spoke with a lawyer today. I'm thinking of filing for divorce."

Once spoken, the D word hung in the air, distended by the silence that stretched between them. Divorce had never been an option in the Wilder clan.

Take Grandma Wilder, Miriam's mother and Rachel's paternal grandmother, a wizened eighty-two-year-old with piercing blue eyes, an iron will, and a rapier tongue. A self-proclaimed "recovering" Irish Catholic, she'd married Grandpa Wilder, an Irish Protestant who, it turned out, had a taste for whiskey. But she'd stuck by him and had borne him five sons and two daughters, in that order. Rachel's father, Peter, was the oldest—a younger, male replica of his mother, who now lived with him in Chicago. Miriam, the youngest, had turned out to be a pint-sized version of her father.

Rachel considered herself a combination of the two women. Like her aunt she sported the Wilder auburn hair and trademark freckles. But, unlike Miriam, she'd been blessed with Grandma Wilder's blue eyes and, through some genetic mutation, a long, sticklike frame that Roger once deemed "willowy."

Miriam cleared her throat. "It's an ill bird that fouls its own nest, dear. If you ask me, it's about time you dumped him."

Relief surged through Rachel, then guilt. "I feel like such a quitter. Do you realize I've been married for eight years?"

"Now, you listen to me, Rachel Wilder Stanhope. You are no quitter," Miriam said, a steely edge creeping into her otherwise lilting voice. "Do you remember the time you took third place in Midwest magazine's Young Photographers competition?"

"I remember the white ribbon hanging on the refrigerator."

"Then you must recall that the following year you went back and took first place, beating out the previous year's winner. That showed tenacity, Rae. Something quitters have little of." Miriam paused. "Things happen in a marriage. Some good, some bad. God knows, if I hadn't outlived my husbands, I'd have left all three."

"With your Puritan ethics?" Rachel rolled her eyes and laughed. "I'm not buying it, Aunt Miriam. But… thanks."

"The point is, sometimes God slams a window. That, my dear, is when you look for the door. Which brings me to why I called."

A sharp rap on her office window snagged Rachel's attention. Jack Jaffery, vice president of design services at Images Plus, stood in the hallway. He knuckled the glass a second time, and gestured sharply toward the conference room. Rachel glanced at the clock, and flashed him the one-minute finger.

"I have to go, Aunt Miriam. Can I call you back?"

"This will take only a second, dear. I have a proposition for you."

Rachel hesitated. Miriam's propositions established the foundations for most of the Wilder family legends. Rachel's father liked to say she was the medium the fairies used to play tricks on unsuspecting people.

"I want you to come and stay at Bird Haven for the summer."

Bird Haven was Miriam's ranch, a 2,500-acre spread that butted against Rocky Mountain National Park, a few miles north of the town of Elk Park, Colorado. She and her late husband, William Tanager, had purchased the property sixteen years ago from a cattle rancher who was closing operations. Once they'd acquired it, they'd designated the land a wild bird sanctuary and converted the barn and outbuildings into a raptor rehabilitation center.

Rachel had spent several summers there as a teenager after her mother died. It was a time of healing—picking wildflowers in the meadow, searching for mountain lion tracks on the deer paths, and wading in the creek running ice-cold with winter runoff. But as much as she loved Bird Haven's back-to-basics pace of life, spending a summer there now was out of the question.

"You're joking, right? You do recall that I have a job, Aunt Miriam?"

One she might lose if she didn't get her rear end into the production meeting soon. Jack, a short, balding man with horn-rimmed glasses and a Sean Connery beard, had the patience of an angry water buffalo. Though Rachel's position as the firm's top creative designer carried some clout, marriage counseling had cut into work time. Pushing Jack much further would be like wearing red in front of an angry bull.

"Just hear me out before you make your decision, Rae. A change of scenery would do you a world of good, and you'd be saving my life."

Jack stuck his head into Rachel's office and jerked his thumb in the air.

"Aunt Miriam, I really don't have time—"

"I have an opportunity to go birding in the Middle East," interrupted Miriam, not the type to be shut down without stating her case. "The problem is, I need to leave someone in charge of things here at the ranch."

"Can't you ask one of the girls?"

William, Miriam's third husband, had brought three daughters from his first marriage into his second. The oldest, Gillian, was an anorexic matron living in Houston with a rocket scientist husband and four children who called Miriam "Nana Rich." The middle daughter, Geraldine, was married to the leader of a South American drug cartel and lived on board a yacht anchored somewhere off the coast of Venezuela. The youngest, Gertrude, lived in Elk Park. Granted, she was somewhat of an energy drain, but she was single and nearing thirty—Rachel's age.

"What about Gertie?"

"I need someone I can trust, dear. With William gone, those girls view me as an interloper. They forget that when we bought this place, your Uncle William and I pooled our resources. He borrowed against his pension, and I chipped in everything I had from my first two marriages. Everything I have is tied up in Bird Haven."

"Can't you just close up the house for a couple of months?"

"It's not that easy, dear. After William died, I turned the operation of the raptor rehabilitation center over to the Park Service, but, per our agreement designating me as the resident landowner, I'm required to have someone on site holding my power of attorney. It's just a formality, in case any unforeseen legal matters pop up. But I also need to leave someone in charge of the checkbook."

That ruled out any of the Tanager sisters. Aunt Miriam's stepdaughters had been hounding her to sell Bird Haven ever since Uncle William had died. He had left them his share of the estate, then tied it up by granting Miriam the right to remain on the property, with a proviso: if she moved, sold out, or remarried, his full share of the land equity at the time of his death was to be divided immediately among his heirs.

"Rachel, those girls are watching my every move. Even a whiff of impropriety could jeopardize the land status. I want a house to come home to."

"What about your attorney? Can't he represent you in your absence?"

Jack loomed at Rachel's door again, his bald head beet red, gleaming like a warning beacon. Rachel nodded before he could bang on the glass.

"My lawyer's the one who recommended I find a family member or friend to stay here. And there just isn't anyone I trust more than you, dear."

"Trust me, I really have to go, Aunt Miriam. I'll call you back." Rachel hung up before her aunt could protest. Then, locating the Henderson folder, she held it up for Jack to see. "Look!"

He jabbed a stubby finger in the direction of the phone. "Keep your personal life out of the office, Rachel. It's interfering with business."

"I'm sorry, Jack."

Tailing her boss to the conference room, Rachel couldn't help but think how Roger had spouted a twisted version of the same sentiment the last time she'd brought work home from the office. He claimed her job interfered with family life—or, more specifically, the business of starting a family.

The production meeting was a regular Monday morning event, and the key players had all assembled by the time Jack and Rachel arrived. There were eleven people present in all— the three other members of the design staff, along with team members from advertising, public relations, and marketing. They all seemed to be tapping their pencils against the conference table in various rhythms of impatience.

"About time," one of the men commented, as Rachel slipped into a vacant chair near the door.

"That's enough, folks. Cut the drumbeat and listen up." Jack ticked off the agenda items with military precision once things got started. They were a quarter of the way through the list and twenty minutes in when the receptionist buzzed. Jack snatched up the receiver, listened, scowled, then told her he didn't care, that even if his mother was in the waiting area, she was not to interrupt them again.

The meeting continued well into a second hour before Rachel was asked to make her presentation. She had spent the previous month designing brochure layouts to promote a Dale Carnegie wanna-be named Kevin Henderson. He offered a series of one-day "Take Back Your Life" seminars and had committed thousands of dollars for a "fresh" brochure design. Then he'd insisted his face beam from every cover, effectively squelching any creative ideas the design staff had come up with.

Ironically, it was Roger who'd triggered the solution. He'd left a packet of reprinted photographs on the coffee table in the living room. The photos, taken over the course of several years, depicted Roger scaling Mount McKinley, biking in the Andes, and participating in a variety of other activities paid for by Rachel's steady employment. A risk junkie from the get-go, Roger openly aspired to try every adventure sport that existed and document his triumphs for posterity. Rachel—exercising latent adolescent genes—had taken a pair of scissors and cut his face out of several of the photographs when inspiration struck. With a little computer technology and some added artistic skill, Kevin Henderson merged with Roger Stanhope and became a man taking his life back.

"The key is in making people feel like once they've attended Henderson's seminar, they can do whatever they dream of doing," explained Rachel, passing out colored examples of her idea. "So, we go ahead and put Kevin on the cover. We show him kayaking a river, caving in New Mexico, lounging on a beach in Puerto Vallarta. We present to the world a person whose troubles are over."

"This is why I put up with you," Jack exclaimed, clapping her on the shoulder once the meeting was over. "You, Ms. Stanhope, have a tendency toward moments of brilliance."

Rachel grimaced. "Does this mean I can call my Aunt Miriam back?"

"Whatever you want," Jack said as they strode away in opposite directions. "Just don't forget, there's a five-minute limit on all personal calls."

Nearing the door to her office, Rachel smelled the scent of cranberry wafting from the potpourri on her bookcase. She sensed the ghost of a shadow imprinted on the room, and peered anxiously inside, half expecting to find someone there. The office was empty, unchanged, except for a manila envelope that lay in the center of her desk. Her name was scrawled across it.

She recognized the handwriting and broke the seal with her fingernail, then gingerly extracted the contents—court documents listing her as Respondent in a Petition for Dissolution of Marriage.

Rachel closed her eyes and cupped a hand over her mouth, afraid of the stinging tears and the sobs threatening to well up from deep in her gut. Anguish was replaced with fleeting denial, then anger. Roger had beaten her to the punch.

She buzzed the receptionist. "Was my husband in the office earlier today?"

The receptionist rushed to explain. "I am so sorry, Rachel. I buzzed the conference room, but Mr. Jaffery yelled at me for interrupting. Your husband said it was okay. He said you weren't expecting him. That maybe it was better this way."

"I'll bet. Thanks." Rachel clicked off and drew a ragged breath. As Respondent, she'd have to respond. As a woman, she just wanted to make sense of the situation. To find the pattern, the order. Had she devoted herself to her job to escape a crumbling relationship, or had her desire to succeed eroded the foundations of her marriage? Were both she and Roger to blame for creating irreconcilable differences, or had she driven him away?

Kevin Henderson's face grinned up from the dummied brochure on her desk. The caption "Take Back Your Life" blared from the page in neon green. Maybe Kevin wasn't as dumb as he looked.

Her thoughts leaped toward Bird Haven and Aunt Miriam's offer. God knew she could use the time away. Plus, Aunt Miriam had always been there for her. Spending the summer in Colorado might be just the ticket. Or, as the saying went, a way to kill two birds with one stone.

Chapter 2

The bird came out of nowhere. A white blur that chirped, then dived, hurtling toward Rachel's head like a B-52 coming in for a hot landing.

She ducked, dropped her suitcase, and swatted at the air above her head. "Get away!"

The bird swerved, then dived again, lighting on the polished mahogany bannister of the entryway. Milk-white and small, it had gray-brown spots forming what looked like a collar around its neck. Its wings and tail feathers were patterned in gray-brown and white; its nose a slash of blue above a yellow beak. The bird cocked its head to one side and eyed her.

"Why, you're some sort of parakeet!" Her words echoed, bouncing off a high ceiling crisscrossed with thick beams. Slatted mahogany shutters flanked tall windows and, to the right, a staircase that looked transported from a Big Valley rerun led to the second floor.

On the left of the stairs, two doorways opened to the interior of the house, but there was no sign of human life anywhere.

"Aunt Miriam?"

No answer. Where the heck was she?

The bird fluttered, spreading its wings from its perch on the bannister. Rachel stared. This was like something out of an Alfred Hitchcock movie. The note taped to the front door had read Come in, dear. 'Beware of Bird' would have been more germane.

Maybe she should try to catch the dumb thing. Rachel's gaze moved toward her suitcase and the handle of the tennis racket protruding from the zipper compartment. Or kill it.

The parakeet stirred.

"Don't even think about it, bird, unless you want to play some modified badminton."

As if in defiance, the parakeet took to the air and settled into a holding pattern above her head. Rachel considered taking the overhead shot, then envisioned Aunt Miriam's reaction. After all, this was a bird sanctuary. Scratch the badminton idea.

"Aunt Miriam? Are you here?"

Still no answer. So much for the cars she'd seen parked out front. Rachel weighed her options. She could wait outside for Aunt Miriam to show up, walk around to the back of the house, or brave the bird.

Rachel sidled toward the front door and the warm rays slanting through the windows. June or not, gooseflesh pimpled her arms. The entryway felt cold. Or maybe she was just in shock.

The parakeet loomed into view like a small bird of prey circling for the kill, and Rachel sucked in a deep breath. She wasn't normally afraid of animals, but she was tired after traveling all day and, she had to admit, the dive-bombing parakeet unnerved her. "Stay away from me, bird."

Perky.

Rachel's gaze followed the parakeet. "Did you say something?"

Perky.

There was no question the bird had spoken, its voice soft and clear. Maybe she could reason with it.

"Is that your name?" she asked.

The parakeet didn't answer.

"All right, Perky, just stay back. I'm not in the mood to play."

No problem, chicky baby.

What a strange bird—and a tenacious one at that. She dodged as Perky swooped past her face. Well, she'd be damned if a nine-inch parakeet was going to stop her from kicking off her shoes and getting comfortable. "Where's Aunt Miriam?"

Miriam, Perky said, buzzing Rachel's head. Her arm arced through the air. Perky slammed against her hand and dropped to the floor.

Rachel stared down at the lifeless bird. He lay on the Navajo rug, wings outspread, feet stiff in the air. My God, she'd killed him. She dropped to her knees and scooped the parakeet into her hands. She hadn't meant to hurt him. She'd just wanted him to leave her alone.

A door creaked at the back of the house, and Rachel's heart

pounded. Aunt Miriam? A few moments ago, Rachel could hardly wait to see her, but now... What was she going to say? "Hi, Aunt Miriam. I killed your bird"?

The parakeet shuddered in Rachel's hands.

Maybe he wasn't dead after all.

She lifted him close to her cheek, willing a whisper of air to pass through his tiny nostrils. She considered giving mouth-to-mouth resuscitation, then dismissed the idea.

But what about CPR? She'd taken a Red Cross first aid class at the office. She must have gleaned something that would apply here.

She brushed a finger over Perky's breast, ruffling his white feathers. The parakeet was about one-twentieth the size of a newborn baby, but where was she supposed to press? If she applied too much pressure, she could crack his chest. Scratch the CPR idea.

Perky jerked.

Was he having a seizure?

The bird twitched, flipped onto his belly, then flew at her face without warning. Sharp claws dug into her scalp. He pecked her head. She felt a sharp tug. Then he flew, landing on a painting high on the wall, an auburn strand of hair dangling from his beak.

"Why, you little beast!"

Perky wants a hair.

"Get somebody else's." Rachel rubbed her head. "Dumb bird."

Stuff it, Perky said. Then he flew away.

Rachel didn't know much about birds, but already she disliked this one.

Picking up her suitcase, Rachel leaned her tennis racket against the wall and set off to find Aunt Miriam. The house looked just as she remembered it. The coat closet, the size of her New York City apartment bedroom and perfect for hiding in during a game of hide-and-seek. The den with its massive desk that looked like Uncle Will had been working there just this morning. The circular bar with its soda fountain. The library with its stacks of books. Everywhere, wood and rock walls, antler chandeliers, and fur rugs mingled with overstuffed leather couches, iron tables, and the occasional William Matthews water-color. Each room boasted a fireplace, burned black over time, now converted to gas. The house smelled of old smoke, burnished wood, new leather—and bird.

At the thought of Perky, Rachel glanced nervously around. Where had the parakeet gone? She was beginning to regret not having had Aunt Miriam meet her at the airport. Instead, she had rented a car, planning for Aunt Miriam to drop it off in two weeks when she left for Cairo.

Rachel had forgotten how treacherous mountain driving could be. Heading toward the snow-capped mountains on the straight ribbon of highway was a piece of cake. But just outside of Loveland, the road made a sharp uphill turn, threading its way through a deep canyon. Steep cliffs of granite rose on either side, boxing in the road and the Big Thompson River. Swollen with runoff, it spread beyond its banks in places, spewing sand and gravel across the blacktop. As the highway climbed from a mile above sea level to over seventy-five hundred feet, Rachel's fingers had clenched the wheel in a death grip. And, now, she was alone in the house with a psycho bird.

"Aunt Miriam? Where are you?"

This time someone answered. "She's outside."

Rachel tracked the voice to the kitchen, half afraid she'd find another talking bird. Instead, a woman about her own age stood at the counter, arranging cheese and meat slices on an oversized platter. Appliances gleamed from granite countertops, and a stainless-steel oven in the corner filled the room with warm, stuffy air.

"I was beginning to think there was no one home except for the parakeet," Rachel said. "What's with that pesky bird, anyway?"

"Rachel Wilder!" the woman exclaimed, setting down a turkey slice. Wiping her palms on her jeans, she extended her hand. Her yellow hair was in a thick braid, and she wore a brightly colored flannel shirt that sparked roses in her cheeks. "I didn't hear you come in."

Rachel glanced at the turkey, thought of salmonella, then

shook the woman's hand. "Stanhope," she corrected. "My name is Rachel Stanhope. And you are…?"

The woman studied her for a moment, then refocused her attention on the platter. "You don't remember me, do you?"

Rachel shook her head. She hadn't been in Elk Park in over four years and didn't know anyone here except Aunt Miriam and Gertie. Rachel refused to believe that her step-cousin—a plump, short, dark-haired woman—had grown into this tall, thin blond. "Should I?"

"I'm Lark."

It took a moment for the information to register. "Lark Drummond?"

The woman nodded.

"I don't believe it!" Rachel hugged her. Lark had been one of Rachel's childhood playmates. Every summer she had stayed with her family at the Drummond Hotel on the north edge of town. A local landmark, the hotel had been built in the early 1900s by one of their ancestors, James Drummond. Rumor was he'd sold the hotel in the 1920s for so much money that none of his family had ever had to work again.

Lark tilted her head. "You've gotten taller. Still, the family resemblance between you and Miriam's amazing."

Rachel fingered her hair. "It's the curse of the Wilder women."

"That's probably why Perky was bugging you," Lark said, offering Rachel a cheese slice. "He loves red hair. He used to drive Miriam crazy. Since her hair's faded some, he leaves her alone."

"I take it he's her bird?"

"Actually, he belonged to William. Or, rather, belonged to a friend of William's. The guy moved out of town. The day he left, he showed up with the bird, dropped him off in a wire cage, and took off."

"I can't say that I blame him."

Lark laughed and shoved the platter toward Rachel. "Help yourself. And don't mind me. I'm just helping Miriam get things set up for later this afternoon."

"What's the occasion?" Rachel asked, hoping nothing had

been planned in honor of her arrival. All she really wanted to do right now was flake out on a couch somewhere and relax.

"Miriam hosts the weekly EPOCH meeting."

"That's right. I forgot."

EPOCH, an acronym for the Elk Park Ornithological Chapter, was the local birdwatchers' club. Miriam had mentioned their Monday meetings when Rachel had called her back about staying at Bird Haven.

The two of them had spent nearly an hour hammering out the terms of the arrangement. Rachel would live at the ranch for the summer, keep an eye on things, and host the weekly EPOCH meetings in Miriam's absence. It was a free ride all around. It got Rachel out of New York City and bought her some much-needed time to figure out what to do about her mess of a life. In return, Miriam got a reliable house sitter and an EPOCH baby-sitter. Besides, how much trouble could a group of blue-haired birdwatchers be?

Rachel's biggest problem had been convincing Jack to let her telecommute from Colorado. He had balked at the idea of having his best designer holed up in some Podunk mountain resort town. He acquiesced only after she'd pointed out that ninety percent of her job involved computer and graphic production work, something she could do by modem. Plus, she'd agreed to fly to New York City anytime the ten percent of the job involving client contact required her presence.

Lark reached for the plastic wrap.

"What time does the EPOCH meeting start?" Rachel asked, plucking one last piece of cheese from the platter.

"Four-thirty-ish. The others should start showing up anytime."

"You mean no one else is here yet?"

Lark shook her head.

"Then who belongs to all the vehicles outside? There have to be at least eight cars out front."

"Most of them belong to hikers."

Did Rachel detect a note of annoyance in Lark's voice? "I take it that's a problem?"

Lark shoved the tray onto the bottom shelf of the refrigerator.

"Only because Miriam's property rests up against Rocky Mountain National Park. Two of the park's trailheads start from here."

"But the park doesn't have public access through Aunt Miriam's land, does it?"

"Not yet. Hikers are supposed to park in the outlying lots, then take the paths skirting the ranch boundaries. Most don't bother. The bottom line is, Miriam needs to install an electronic gate at the end of the driveway, pronto, and start having the cars towed."

"Just for a few extra parking spaces?" Rachel didn't think it was worth the hassle.

"That's not the point," Lark said. "Bird Haven's allowed free access for better than sixteen years. One more year and the road becomes a permanent public access by Colorado law."

Which would create a change in land status. It was definitely not in Aunt Miriam's best interests to ignore the situation. Rachel studied Lark and wondered if she knew about the stipulations of Uncle Will's trust, or if she was just looking out for Miriam.

Rachel decided to change the subject until she could discuss the situation with Miriam, "So what brings you back to Elk Park? Just here on vacation?"

"Nope, I'm a full-time resident now," Lark said, busying herself with the coffeemaker. "About three years ago the Drummond came up for sale. I'd always dreamed of owning it, bringing it back into the family, so to speak. All it took was the flick of a pen and… voilà!" Lark spread her arms wide. "I went from trust-funder to working stiff. You are looking at the current proprietor of the Drummond Hotel and Convention Center."

"Congratulations." *Talk about taking back your life!* Rachel stood up and kneaded the muscle tension in her lower back. "I think I could use a walk after the trip up here. Did you say Aunt Miriam was outside?"

"Yep."

"Do you think I have time to find her before the meeting starts?"

"I don't see why not, seeing as she's the one who starts the meeting." Lark gestured toward the back door. "She's showing some reporter the rehab center."

The Raptor House was visible from the back patio. Headquartered in a green barn shoved into a clump of Douglas firs, it stood some 300 yards from the house. She crossed the yard, where sprigs of Indian paintbrush and fuzzy pasque flowers poked through the grass. Birds twittered from the treetops.

Rachel breathed in the pine-spiced air and thought back to the last time she'd seen her aunt. Miriam had flown to New York, stayed two days, and left. Uncle Will had died three weeks later.

Rachel felt the familiar stab of guilt; the kind time doesn't erase. The kind time never lets you forget. Focused on her career, she hadn't attended Uncle Will's funeral, leaving Aunt Miriam to grieve alone. What was it that Grandma Wilder always said? "You can't mend torn underwear." Well, she might be right about that, but Rachel intended to try.

The doors of the barn stood partially open. Rachel heard angry voices and stopped at the threshold.

"You can't really believe William had anything to do with what happened to those falcons."

Rachel recognized the voice as Miriam's.

"Why shouldn't I believe that, Mrs. Tanager? Everything I've uncovered points to his guilt. Now that he's dead, I'd hoped you'd be willing to share what you know. Or maybe you're hiding something, too."

"I've listened to enough of your prattle. I want you to leave."

"Why? Because I've uncovered a scheme you don't want your bird friends knowing about? One way or another, it's all coming out."

Rachel stepped from the sunlight into a large barn lined with cages. A one-winged bald eagle perched on an aspen stand, tethered to a stake anchored in the center of the earthen floor. Agitated, it opened and snapped its beak shut several times.

"Is everything all right?" she asked.

"Rae!" Miriam stepped toward her. The standard version of a

Wilder woman, Miriam was small-boned and stood all of five-two. Her red hair and freckles were faded by age, but her hazel eyes shone dark with anger. "This is Mr. Bursau. He was just leaving."

Ignoring Rachel, the reporter stood hunched over Miriam, his shoulders drawn to his ears like a vulture poised over carrion. "You don't really want to send me away, Mrs. Tanager. You know as well as I that this story deserves to be told."

"Perhaps so, Mr. Bursau. But they won't hear it from me." The tension in Miriam's voice was palpable. The tethered eagle stretched, flapping its wing.

Bursau spun on his heel and pushed past Rachel, slamming the barn door into the siding. Birds screeched in annoyance. "Some of these people are dangerous, Mrs. Tanager," he called from the doorway. "If I were you, I'd watch my back." Then he was gone.

Miriam sighed. Her face relaxed, and she straightened the hem of her sweater before speaking. "What a perfectly despicable man."

"Who was he?"

"Donald Bursau, a reporter for *Birds of a Feather* magazine. Someone worth putting out of your mind." Miriam soothed the eagle, then turned and hugged Rachel. "Now, let's have a look at you. I'm so happy you're here."

Rachel returned Miriam's hug, but remained curious about the reporter. "What story was he talking about?"

Miriam shook her head. "The man has some insane notion that your Uncle William was involved in some wild bird trafficking scheme. Something that took place years ago." Miriam swiped her hand through the air and turned away. "He's simply crazy."

The fact that Miriam had busied herself with the eagle and wouldn't look her in the eye aroused Rachel's suspicions.

"He seemed pretty sincere about his warning."

"He may believe some of William's associates are involved. He may even believe some are dangerous. But I say he's full of bird doo."

Rachel had met a few of William Tanager's colleagues, a group of ornithologists who at their worst might be accused of boring a non-birder to sleep. They certainly didn't seem like dangerous individuals. At least not by most people's definition.

"What do you say we drop the subject, Rachel? After all, you've just arrived." Miriam linked arms with her niece and guided her toward the open barn doors. "I assume you saw Lark in the kitchen."

"I did," Rachel said, not quite ready to change the topic of conversation. "Getting back to—"

"She's such a wonderful girl."

"Aunt Miriam!"

"I just know you're going to become fast friends again."

Rachel threw up her hands. "Okay, you win." There wasn't much she could do if Aunt Miriam refused to discuss her conversation with the reporter. "But I reserve the right to bring it up later."

"Done," Miriam said, unlinking her arm from Rachel's. She brushed her hands together. "Now that that's settled, help me lock up. We'll go out the back, so I can make one stop on the way to the house. And we'll need to hurry, dear. We don't want to be late."

"Late for what?"

"The EPOCH meeting."

Rachel had forgotten all about it. Well, it was too late to beg off now.

Once the barn doors were secure, Miriam led Rachel between two rows of caged birds, through a room furnished like a veterinarian's surgical area, and out the rear door. The center hadn't been complete the last time Rachel was here. In fact, they'd only just finished the conversion of the old barn. Now a maze of covered walkways linked the barn to six large outbuildings.

"What are all these buildings used for?"

Miriam waved at the barn behind them. "Where we just were, is the intensive care unit. The rest of the buildings house birds being readied for release." She pointed to the farthest one on the right and ticked them off in order. "That's the Nesting Compound for burrowing owls. Freedom House is where the birds get their final test flights before being returned to the wild.

The Pygmy House shelters the smaller owls and the kestrels. The Eagles' Eyrie speaks for itself, and Protective Custody House is the hospital ward."

"Where are we headed?"

"Collegiate Hall, the educational wing." Miriam unlocked the door, stepped into a cramped hallway and flipped on a dim, overhead light. "The cages in all the buildings come equipped with a type of double-door entry system, to help prevent accidental releases. The inside walls have narrow cuts in them for observation."

Rachel cupped her hands over her nose. The air inside smelled of bird, damp wood, and thawed meat. Rachel forced herself to follow Miriam, cringing as the door clicked shut behind them.

"Collegiate Hall has seven cages," Miriam continued. "Down here, at the end, we have two juvenile peregrine falcons. Their mother was shot and killed in the park, when they were barely a week old."

Miriam stopped, and Rachel pressed her face close to the observation slits, grateful for the soft movement of air. "Isn't it illegal to shoot falcons?"

"Of course, dear, but that doesn't stop anyone. We were just lucky to find the eyasses before they starved to death or were eaten by predators."

Rachel peered through the slit into a cage the size of a living room. It was constructed of solid wood panels on one side and of cedar slats one inch apart on the other. Ankle-deep vegetation grew up from the earthen floor. She waited for her eyes to adjust to the light, then sought out the birds. Downy white and robin-sized, they perched on the edge of a makeshift cliff nest.

"They're a lot smaller than I expected," she said. "How old are they?"

"Around three weeks." Miriam fumbled with the latch on the inside door. "We're moving them to a hacking box next week."

"I hate to sound ignorant, Aunt Miriam, but what is that?"

A smile flickered across her aunt's face. "It's a wooden platform, dear. It's set in a protected area where the eyasses are kept until they fledge. We prefer placing orphans with adults who have wild young of a similar age, but in this case it wasn't possible."

"Like foster parenting for birds?"

"Exactly."

The latch gave with a sharp click. The nestlings hissed.

"Once they've hacked, we'll continue to feed them until they acquire the necessary skills to survive on their own and migrate." Miriam approached the nest. The eyasses cackled, and one struck out with its foot.

"Feisty little things," Rachel said.

"Yes, but they still have to learn how to hunt and protect themselves."

"From what? Aren't they at the top of the food chain?"

"Close, though they're sometimes targeted by other raptors. Once these juveniles fly, their risks diminish, but then there are other dangers to face."

"Such as?"

"The biggest threat," Miriam said, pulling a package of food from her pocket, "is man."

Chapter 3

Miriam ripped open the plastic seal on the package, pulled out several long strips of raw meat, and tossed them to the young falcons. "The big ways are obvious. Habitat encroachment, pesticide usage, that sort of thing."

"And...?" Rachel prompted, convinced that Miriam was leaving something unsaid. Miriam flung another piece of meat onto the feeding board.

"And, up until fifteen years ago, there was a huge international market for peregrines for falconries overseas."

The young birds tore at the raw flesh, staining their beaks and feathers red. Rachel's stomach churned. "What happened fifteen years ago? Did the market just dry up?"

"The government cracked down, and people started breeding the birds in captivity. Reintroduction of the peregrines has been so successful the government is considering delisting them."

Now for the million-dollar question. "So how does this tie in with Donald Bursau's article?"

Miriam jerked her head up and stared at Rachel, hazel eyes darkening. "He thinks your uncle William was involved in the disappearance of an adult peregrine and her eyas from the park in 1984. I told him that was absurd, that your uncle William was a renowned ornithologist, top in his field, who devoted a lifetime to the protection and study of birds. I refuse to let some overzealous reporter go and spoil all that."

"Does Bursau have any proof to back up his allegations?"

Miriam kicked at the ankle-deep grass growing on the floor of the falcons' cage. Blood poured from the bag in her hand, dampening the blades. "He claims to, but he wouldn't share it with me. Frankly, I think he's bluffing."

The questions were obviously upsetting Miriam. Rachel considered dropping the subject again, but there was no way she could help unless she knew what was going on. "How does he think Uncle William acquired the birds?"

"Bursau claims the birds were brought into the Raptor House

for treatment, then disappeared." Miriam stepped into the hallway and pulled the cage door shut. "I told him it wasn't possible. William ran a tight ship, and we kept records on every bird brought in."

"What kind of records?"

"Accurate ones." Miriam's hands trembled as she reached for the handle on the outside door. "The treatment a bird receives, how long it's here, when it's released, is all documented."

Rachel stepped outside, squinting in the bright sunlight. She gulped fresh air, feeling freed herself.

She knew from previous discussions with Miriam that nearly ninety-three percent of the birds treated at Raptor House survived. Unfortunately, not all ended up fit for release back to the wild. "What happens if a bird can't be rehabilitated?"

Miriam fiddled with the door lock. "Around twenty to thirty percent of the birds end up in educational programs, like Isaac, the eagle you saw in the barn."

"So all of the birds get placed somewhere." It was nice to know that with a little help from the species annihilating them, the majority of the birds survived.

A shadow crossed Miriam's face. "Unfortunately, we can't always find programs for the more seriously injured."

"What happens to them?"

"They're euthanized, dear."

A few minutes later, Rachel found herself seated on the patio off the kitchen with a glass of pink lemonade clutched in her hand. Lark had dragged a chair up beside her. The seven other attendees pulled their seats into a semicircle around Aunt Miriam.

Gertie arrived just as the EPOCH meeting officially came to order. Rachel nodded at her. Gertie shrugged in response.

"First," Miriam said, gesturing toward Rachel, "I'd like to introduce my niece. She'll be staying at Bird Haven while I'm gone. And the good news is, she's agreed to host the weekly EPOCH meetings."

Rachel smiled, acknowledging the brief round of applause following Miriam's announcement. As a whole, the gathered birdwatchers bore little resemblance to the elderly gaggle Rachel had envisioned. Ranging in age from thirty-something to their mid-sixties, they made up more of a middle-aged gaggle.

"I think we should go around and introduce ourselves," Gertie said. She'd situated herself on the other side of Lark, scrunching her extra-wide fanny onto the medium-sized chair. She still wore her dark hair cropped short, and with her pug nose, she looked like an overfed Boston terrier. "I'll start even though, being cousins by marriage, Rachel knows me. FYI, I'm also EPOCH's newsletter editor. It's nice to see you."

"Ditto," Rachel said, mustering little enthusiasm.

Lark grinned and elbowed her in the ribs. "We've met, so I'll pass."

The next person in line pointed to the woman beside her. "This is my sister, Cecilia Meyer. She's our treasurer. I'm Dorothy MacBean. Welcome to Elk Park."

The women bobbed their heads in rhythm, like two Taco Bell chihuahuas. Both had pale skin, gray eyes, and stylishly permed hair. Rachel wondered if they were twins. If they weren't, their family resemblance rivaled that of the Wilder women. Accessory color seemed to be their only distinguishing feature. Dorothy wore pink. Cecilia wore blue.

A straight-backed man sitting beside Miriam leaned forward. He looked vaguely familiar to Rachel, his short, gray hair complimenting a pair of ice-blue eyes. He sported a small diamond stud in his left earlobe. "Charles Pendergast, here. I was a childhood friend of your Uncle Will's. Actually, I believe we've met before." He reached over and patted Miriam's knee. "I've known your aunt quite a long time."

Rachel noticed the tip of his right index finger was missing, then averted her eyes, wondering if her aunt returned his obvious interest. He wasn't the first man to set his sights on the widow. God knew, Aunt Miriam could take care of herself.

"I'm Forest Nettleman," the man beside Charles declared. He stood, and squeezed Rachel's hand in a firm grip. "U.S. Representative for the 4th District. We're pleased to have you with us, very pleased. And we're glad to know that you've agreed to host our meetings in your aunt's absence. I don't just speak for myself when I say we hope you're planning to join us on some of our birding adventures. We have quite an active club here in Elk Park. We pride ourselves on—"

"Thank you, Forest," interjected Miriam. She quickly introduced the last two members of the group, Andrew and Opal Henderson, a couple who lived in a small town down the valley. Andrew, who must have weighed four hundred pounds, had a balding pate and wispy goatee. Opal looked undernourished, and wore her thick, dull hair piled high on her head.

The introductions completed, Miriam turned to the first order of business, a motion to approve the minutes of the last meeting. Gertie's hand shot up.

"There's an error in the second line of paragraph four that needs correction, Miriam. Towhee was misspelled."

"Thank you, Gertie. Anything else?" Miriam glanced around the circle. "No? Then will someone please make a motion?"

"I move we accept the minutes," Dorothy said.

"Do I have a second?"

"I'll second," Lark said.

"Thank you. Discussion? All in favor? Opposed? The minutes are approved."

Rachel listened as Miriam conducted the meeting in a fashion that would have garnered approval from the Robert of Robert's Rules of Order. With a businesslike formality reminiscent of Images Plus, Miriam heard from whom she wanted, keeping Gertie on a tight leash at all times.

"All right, then, we're down to new business."

Gertie raised her hand.

"Yes?" Miriam clearly was exasperated.

"I had a message on my voice mail this morning from a Donald Bursau. For those of you who don't know who he is, he's a reporter from Birds of a Feather magazine. He was asking to set up an interview regarding Daddy. His message indicated he was coming out to talk with you this afternoon, Miriam." Gertie's hands fluttered in the air. "Did he?"

Miriam glanced at Rachel, then nodded. "Yes, he was here."

"It sounded to me like he plans to do a feature story on my

father."

Rachel avoided her cousin's gaze. Gertie seemed excited. Obviously the content of his story remained unknown to her. She must think Bursau was planning a favorable piece.

"I'm not sure what he's going to write, Gertie," Miriam said. "He was asking a lot of questions about the Raptor House operation. I referred him to Eric."

"He must have given some indication of what he planned to do." Gertie held up a full-color, glossy magazine, and panned it in front of the EPOCH members. "You must all realize that Donald Bursau isn't just any reporter. He's the Geraldo Rivera of the bird world. If he's interested in doing an article on my father and the Raptor House, we should all be included. After all, we helped build the rehabilitation center. It would be good publicity for our group. And, for that matter, Elk Park in general."

"As I said, Gertie, I referred him to Eric." Miriam pushed back a strand of hair and forced a smile. "Now is there any other new business before we adjourn? If not, then will someone please move—"

"Hold on." A tall man had stepped around the corner of the house and jogged toward them. His brown hair was clipped short around the ears, barely brushing the collar of his rumpled Park Ranger uniform. Dark glasses obscured his eyes, and long, tanned legs disappeared into a pair of oatmeal socks and hiking boots.

"Well, speak of the devil." Gertie grinned smugly. "Maybe I'll get an answer to my questions."

Rachel nudged Lark. "Who's he?"

"Eric Linenger, the ranger assigned to the Raptor House. Not to mention, Elk Park's most eligible bachelor." Her expression said she'd auditioned for the girlfriend role, and hadn't gotten a callback.

"What is it, Eric? Is something wrong?" Miriam turned toward the Raptor House. Rachel conjured an image of the baby peregrines hissing.

"No, everything's fine," he said in a thick Scandinavian accent. "But a group of birders just spotted a LeConte's sparrow down at The Thicket."

A hum rose from the membership.

"Are you sure? Has the sighting been confirmed?" Charles Pendergast slid to the edge of his chair, his fingers tapping on the armrest.

"Ja. Harry Eckles is down there now. He verified the identification."

"Harry is another regular member," Lark whispered. "A biology professor at the University of Colorado in Boulder. He's one guy who knows his species." She pulled a small book from her pocket, thumbed to the picture of a multicolored bird, then pointed to a small map colored in purples and pinks. "This is the range map."

"We can't believe it," Dorothy exclaimed, apparently speaking for herself and Cecilia. "The LeConte's sparrow is practically unheard of in these parts."

Cecilia nodded.

"But it's here," Eric said.

"This is one for my life list," Nettleman declared. "How about the rest of you?"

Hands shot up. Pendergast stood. The hum grew louder.

"What's a life list?" Rachel asked.

"A birdwatcher's record." Lark pulled a folder from her pocket and handed it over. "It's a checklist of all the birds you spot in a lifetime."

"Order!" Aunt Miriam demanded, pounding her fist on the table. The clamor of excited voices dwindled to a respectful buzz. "That's better. Now, I know this is exciting, but we need to stay calm and organized. The first thing we should do is call the other members."

Rachel leaned closer to Lark. "How many more are there?"

"Forty or so. Only about fifteen are active, and only about half of those show up." Lark slapped her thigh. "The rest are probably down at The Thicket. Darn! I should have known something was up when Harry didn't show up for the meeting."

"Hush!" Miriam glared at Lark and Rachel. Several of the others slid back their chairs and stood. Miriam waved them back down. "I know everyone's anxious, but...has someone notified the hot line?"

"Ja, Harry called it in."

"That means Elk Park is under an official rare bird alert," Gertie said, her shrill voice rising to a shriek.

"It looks that way," Eric agreed.

"What happens now?" Rachel asked.

Lark shrugged. "We all race down to The Thicket and hope the bird is still there. If we miss it, we stake out the area, hoping it shows up again."

"Won't we scare it off, racing down there en masse?"

"Let's hope not. There are a lot of people, like me, who would kill for a look at that bird."

Chapter 4

The LeConte's sparrow hissed at dusk. At least, Rachel hoped it was the sparrow. They'd been looking for it the past three days, scouring The Thicket, fanning out in all directions. She had begged off on Tuesday and Wednesday, claiming work as an excuse, but today Aunt Miriam's request held more insistence and Rachel had acquiesced. She was, after all, a guest.

The bird hissed again, and she peered in the direction of the sound, surprised by how quickly the sky had dimmed once the sun started dropping behind Long's Peak. Similar to the way the lights dimmed in a fancy restaurant when the menu prices went up after dark.

And, the temperature was dropping. Rachel pulled her hands inside the cuffs of her long-sleeved shirt, chastising herself for not bringing a jacket. Earlier in the day, the temperature had reached a balmy seventy-two. Why did Elk Park nights always offer an opportunity for hypothermia?

A rustle in the bushes behind her caused her to stop and glance back. The Thicket was tangled and dense. Comprised mostly of willows, alder, and ankle- to knee-high grasses, it stretched a quarter-mile or more along the river-bank, blocking the view of Black Canyon Creek. A second rustle set Rachel's heart pounding.

Stay calm, Stanhope, she ordered herself. It's just a bird. Maybe the bird.

Rachel focused her attention on the book Aunt Miriam had shoved into her hands as they left the house. The book described the LeConte's sparrow as "smaller than a House Sparrow, bright buff-ochre eyebrow stripe, buffy breast and sides, white belly, gray nape with purple streaks, black crown with whitish crown stripe, orange face surrounding gray cheek, and dark and light streaking on back," whatever that meant. It would be Rachel's first official sighting.

According to Aunt Miriam and Lark, the American Birding

Association's life list consisted of nine hundred and six wild bird species, of which Rachel could positively identify two— the American robin and the bald eagle. She'd already mistaken the common raven for a crow.

A twig snapped, and Rachel whipped her head around. Since when could a bird break off tree branches?

Two weeks ago, Aunt Miriam had said, she'd spotted a mountain lion in the area. The cat had come down to the water to drink. They'd eyed each other, then gone their separate ways.

Sightings weren't all that uncommon. Lions ranged as far east as the suburbs of Denver. With man's encroachment on their territory, the number of sightings had jumped, along with an increase in the number of attacks. Last year, one in Rocky Mountain National Park had resulted in the death of a nine-year-old.

The thought caused Rachel's heart to bang against her ribs. What if it wasn't the sparrow she'd been hearing?

A pamphlet she'd picked up yesterday at the park's ranger station stated that mountain lions were active day and night, feeding on mule deer and large rodents. It had noted four major things to remember if you came upon a lion in the wild: stay calm, look big, talk loud, and back away slowly.

Calm was impossible. Control? Maybe. Rachel drew a deep breath.

Looking big was easy. At five-foot-seven and 130 pounds, Rachel dwarfed the average porcupine.

Loud she could also handle. In fact, she planned to yell her head off at the first sign of a tawny, catlike creature.

But backing away slowly presented a real problem. Her ingrained response to fear was flight, which was what had brought her to Elk Park in the first place.

Rachel drew a second deep breath and straightened her shoulders. Chances were it was just someone from the group ahead of her who had doubled back.

"Hello?" she called.

No answer.

"Hello? Anyone there?"

Another crackling from The Thicket sent her scrambling up

the deer path. Seven people, including Aunt Miriam, were ahead of her. As Miriam would say, it's the dead duck that flies at the end of the line. If it was a mountain lion in The Thicket, Rachel wanted to be in the middle of the pack. If it was the sparrow, there ought to be someone around who could identify the darned thing.

The first person Rachel overtook was Lark. "I heard something back there," she whispered.

Lark held a finger to her lips. "Where?"

"In the bushes," Rachel said, wondering why they were whispering. "It hissed, but then I heard some branches crack and—"

"It hissed?" Lark looped her binoculars around her neck. "How far back were you?"

Rachel pointed toward Black Canyon Creek.

"Come on." Lark moved along the deer path, and Rachel hesitated, unsure she wanted to backtrack in that direction.

"It was making a lot of noise. What if it wasn't a bird?"

Lark stopped and turned, her long braid flipping from one shoulder to the other. "Cut to the chase. What are you really scared of?"

"What if it was something else, like that mountain lion Aunt Miriam saw?"

Lark emitted a hoot. "Mountain lions don't hiss at people."

"I know that," Rachel said in a stage whisper. "But I also can't believe a secretive little sparrow that likes weeds and grass would make that much noise in the bushes."

"Okay, so the bush-cracker was probably a squirrel or a rabbit, but the hissing sounds like the sparrow. So can we go?" Lark started back down the path toward Black Canyon Creek, arms swinging. "I can see I'm going to have to teach you a thing or two."

Rachel hung back. How much she needed to learn from Lark hinged directly on how much time she intended to spend birdwatching. Likely very little. Once Aunt Miriam left for the Middle East, Rachel planned to enjoy the mountains from the back deck. Another rare bird alert, and even going home to Roger might start looking good.

When Lark disappeared around a bend in the path, Rachel considered her options. Seek out Aunt Miriam and the others, stick with Lark, or stand around like mountain lion bait.

Uphill, the path wound through a pine forest before rejoining The Thicket on the other side of the knoll. The trees pressed close together, their branches blocking out light on even a sunny day. Behind her, the meadow still captured the last of the day's rays. The choice was a no-brainer.

The rocky trail toward Black Canyon Creek narrowed in places, and was slick with mud in others. Rachel picked her way down more slowly than she'd climbed. It took her a few minutes to catch up to Lark.

"Where were you when you heard the hissing?" whispered Lark.

Rachel pointed to a spot farther down the path. "Somewhere in there."

Lark placed a finger to her lips, and waved Rachel closer. "Lesson number one: be quiet. The bird'll hide if you're too noisy. Or it'll fly away. In the case of the LeConte's, it runs, using the grass for cover."

Did Lark actually believe she wanted to become a world-class birdwatcher? Think again.

A weak song erupted from the brush, and Lark cocked her head. "I think it is the LeConte's sparrow. Man, if it's back there in the grasses, it'll be bird number 497."

"Great," Rachel said, trying to muster some enthusiasm. She didn't understand the excitement. After all, a bird was a bird, right? These people acted like the sparrow was a rare treasure.

"LeContes skulk in the grass. They stay close to the ground," explained Lark, peering through her binoculars. She crouched low, trying to see around the bushes, performing gyrations befitting an acrobat. "I can't see anything. We're going to have to pish it out."

"Pish? That's a Yiddish word for pee! You're not planning to do anything weird, are you?"

"Of course not." Lark squinted up at the crown of light over Long's Peak. "In birder talk, it means we're going to make pishing noises in order to draw the bird out of The Thicket. And we need to hurry, before we run out of sunlight."

"Why not just shake the bushes, stomp our feet, and scare the thing out?"

"Because that goes against birdwatching etiquette! The American Birding Association's Code of Birding Ethics clearly states that a birder should never deliberately disturb a bird's habitat."

Rachel raised her hands in mock surrender. "I was only asking."

"This isn't a joke. It's considered bad form. We either have to lure it out, or wait." Lark lifted her binoculars and scanned the brush again. "Tell me again what it sounded like."

"It hissed."

Lark hung her binoculars around her neck by their strap, and placed her hands on her hips. "Get with the program, Rae. Can you imitate its call or not?"

She could whistle for a cab, so why not hiss?

A sharp squeak erupted on her first attempt. She pressed a knuckle to her lips, quelling a laugh. This was absurd!

Lark shifted her weight from one foot to the other.

"Okay, just give me a second." Rachel wrinkled her nose, replayed the call in her head, and tried again. Kshshsh.

Lark tried. "Like that?"

"Close. Drawl it out a little more. Like Kshshshshshs."

Lark practiced a couple of times, then steered Rachel toward the willow thicket and the creek. "You go around this way. I'll double back on the other side. Hiss as you walk, and keep your eyes open. What we're hoping for is that the bird'll get curious and pop its head up to see what all the racket's about."

"Lark, I don't—"

"Just go." Lark pushed her off the trail.

Rachel skirted the edge of The Thicket, afraid to consider what other kinds of wildlife might be lurking about.

The ground was boggy in places, and the closer she came to the creek, the deeper her feet sank into mud. She heard Lark hissing and, in spite of feeling ridiculous, issued an occasional hiss in reply. No answering calls issued from The Thicket.

Water seeped through the stitching of her shoes. Her socks

grew damp. Her feet grew cold. A light winked on in the window of the Raptor House, perched high on the rise. Dusk settled deep into the valley. In another ten minutes they'd be forced to call off the search for lack of light, which suited Rachel fine.

She stepped carefully over a fallen log as she rounded the back of the jumble of willows, white alder, and tufted hairgrass, catching her sock on a twig. She bent to loosen it, and her fingertips brushed something squishy and cool. She yanked her hand back and stared hard into the tangle of branches and grasses. In the dwindling light, she made out a body, facedown.

Blood rushed to her head. Her ears roared.

Don't scream, Stanhope. Don't scream. The first thing to do was see if the person was breathing. She bent closer.

By the size of the figure she knew it was the body of a man, his fingers curled against a mossy rock. She tried to roll him over, but he stayed wedged among the branches of The Thicket. Rachel checked his wrist for a pulse, repelled by the clamminess and mottled texture of the man's skin.

He was dead, definitely dead.

"Lark," she yelled, thrashing her way toward the river. "Lark."

Kshshsh.

"Lark!"

"Quit yelling, Rae!" Lark ordered in a stage whisper from the other side of the bushes. Kshshsh.

Rachel pushed through The Thicket in the direction of Lark's voice. Branches snapped. In a rush of feathers, two birds rose from the brush. A large raven flapped away toward Lumpy Ridge, a final ray of sunlight dancing off its legs and the catch in its beak. A smaller, multicolored bird lit momentarily on an exposed branch, cocked its head, then settled back into The Thicket grasses.

"Did you see that?" Lark pointed with vigor at the bush. "It was the LeConte's sparrow! I got bird number 497."

Rachel reached her in two bounding steps and gripped her shoulders tightly. "Listen to me."

"Did you see it?" Lark pumped her arms up and down like a

hyperactive child. "Did you see it?"

"It doesn't matter." Rachel dragged Lark forward. "You have to follow me."

"What do you mean it doesn't matter? Of course it matters."

"Lark, please!"

"What's going on down there?" Aunt Miriam's voice wafted from higher ground, somewhere near the deer path. "Did you spot the sparrow?"

Rachel clamped her hand across Lark's mouth, allowing only a muffled response and sticking her face nose-to-nose with the startled woman. "Lark, I found a body."

"Well, will someone answer? Have you seen it?" The second voice belonged to Charles Pendergast.

Rachel pulled her hand away from Lark's mouth. "Did you hear me?"

Lark nodded, her blond braid seesawing across her shoulder, her mouth gaping.

"Is it still there?" Gertie called out, her voice rising above the others, her words tumbling over one another in excitement. "Which side of the tangle is it on?"

So much for being quiet. Rachel ignored the volley of questions from the gathering birdwatchers and dragged Lark around the edge of The Thicket. "It's over here."

"What did you say, dear?" Miriam's voice sounded closer.

"Stay back, Aunt Miriam," Rachel ordered. "All of you, stay back. I found a body down here. Someone needs to go and call the police."

"Did she say 'a body'?"

"Yes, Gertie, a body. A dead person."

"Oh, heavens," Dorothy and Cecilia said in unison.

With a clamor that defied birding etiquette, the bird-watchers stormed the bush. Rachel fervently hoped they wouldn't trample the corpse.

"Everyone, stop where you are!"

Rachel didn't recognize the stern, male voice. A tremor of fear shot through her. She grabbed Lark's sleeve. The man was between them and the others. Did he have some connection to the body in the bush?

Rachel slipped around a twisting willow to get a closer look. Wrestling with a branch, she stepped forward and bumped smack into a tall, muscular man. His jeans and navy blue fleece jacket blended so well with the twilight that he faded into The Thicket.

"Excuse me." He extended his arm, blocking Rachel's forward progress. "I said, 'Stop.'"

Rachel stood her ground, shivering from shock and cold. She groped for Lark's arm, then realized her friend was no longer behind her. Where had she gone?

The bushes parted, and Miriam and Charles stepped into the small clearing.

"Harry," Miriam said, exhaling audibly. She nodded to Rachel. "Harry's a member of EPOCH."

Rachel's fear ebbed slightly despite her growing concern for Lark's whereabouts. Harry was the biology professor, "the guy who knew his species." Rachel wondered if he knew anything about dead people. She pointed toward the thick tangle of willows to the west. "The body's over there."

A murmur rose from the gathering crowd. Gertie lifted her binoculars to her face. A scream pierced the air. Lark stood ten yards away, staring down at the ground.

Harry covered the distance in a few long strides. Rachel scrambled behind, twigs snapping underfoot, branches scraping her ankles.

He brushed past Lark, and Rachel stopped. She draped an arm around Lark's shoulders and pulled her away, glad to have an excuse not to move any closer. When Harry squatted to examine the body and played the beam from his flashlight over the man's profile, Rachel gasped.

Donald Bursau lay facedown, dead in the mud.

Chapter 5

"I know this man," Rachel said, shocked. If you take away the blue tinge. Maybe he should have heeded his own warning. What if Aunt Miriam really was in danger?

"It looks like he's been shot." Harry rose from his haunches. "Everybody needs to stay back."

Lark jerked away from the crowd, moving uphill. A few seconds later Rachel heard her retching in the bushes.

"Did he say 'shot'?" Gertie asked. She edged forward, her birdwatcher's vest flapping open to reveal a pink sweatshirt with a hand-painted bluebird pecking one breast.

"This is terrible," Dorothy cried, clutching her sister's arm. "Stay back from there, Cecilia."

Charles gently steered Aunt Miriam away from the clearing. "Come on, let's go back up on the path."

"What's going on?"

The owner of the voice was Eric Linenger. He materialized with Forest Nettleman in tow, scaring Rachel nearly to death.

Gertie grabbed his arm. "Oh, Eric, it's awful! They found a body."

"What? Who?" he asked. "Does anyone know who it is?"

The birdwatchers turned en masse, staring at Rachel. Shoot! She was hoping no one had heard her declaration. She wanted a chance to talk with Aunt Miriam before answering any questions.

"It's Donald Bursau, the reporter from Birds of a Feather magazine." She glanced at Miriam. Her aunt's eyes seemed to urge secrecy.

"No!" Gertie pushed forward, her voice a wail. "It can't be!"

"Why would anyone want to kill him?" asked Forest.

Gertie whirled on Miriam, her face scrunched with anger. "Maybe we should be asking Miriam that question."

"What are you talking about, Gertie?" Charles demanded, placing a protective arm around Miriam's shoulders.

"I know for a fact that she was one of the last people in Elk

Park to talk with Donald Bursau."

"So? Big deal!" scoffed Charles.

Gertie turned and addressed the rest of the birdwatchers. "I tried returning his call on Tuesday morning, to schedule the interview he'd requested, and the hotel clerk told me he'd checked out on Monday evening. According to the clerk, Mr. Bursau seemed extremely agitated. Then he received a telephone call and his mood changed. He agreed to meet someone, then left, just like that." She snapped her fingers.

Miriam pinched her lower lip between her teeth and leaned against Charles. Rachel frowned. What did Aunt Miriam know about that call?

"I still don't see what you're getting at, Gertie," Charles said, patting Miriam's arm. "He was obviously alive after he left Bird Haven. You're such a prattling buzzard sometimes."

"Who are you calling a buzzard, you sixties reprobate?"

"That's enough," Eric said. "The first thing we need to do is deal with the present situation. I want everyone to move away from the crime scene. And someone needs to go call the sheriff."

At the mention of calling someone, Rachel remembered the cell phone clipped to her belt. Standard issue at Images Plus, she never knew when it would come in handy. "Here, Eric. You can use this."

"You dial," he said, herding them all toward the deer path. "Now everyone listen up. We need to stop talking about this. The sheriff will want to hear from each of us, not a group version of what happened."

Rachel moved a few feet away and punched in 911. She explained the situation to the dispatcher, and was told to stay on the line.

Around her the night had grown quiet. The sun had dropped behind the mountains, shrouding The Thicket in darkness. The birdwatchers clustered in silence. There were no horns blaring, people shouting, or cars whizzing past on busy streets. Out here the wind rustled the willows, night birds called from the meadow, and the creek babbled over stones as it wound its way toward Elk Lake. Chief Joseph's line in Little Big Man sprang to mind: "It's a good day to die."

Cecilia Meyer's voice shattered the tranquillity, and Rachel realized it was the first time she'd ever heard her speak. "I suppose this means The Thicket will be off-limits for a while," she said. "It seems a shame."

"Cecilia!" Dorothy said. "A man is dead."

"Yes, but did anyone see the bird?"

A murmuring rose from the birdwatchers.

Rachel's head ached. She wanted a chance to talk with Aunt Miriam—alone—before the sheriff arrived and started asking questions. She figured Aunt Miriam might be able to shed some light on why Bursau was murdered. Or who might have murdered him. But would she implicate herself in the process?

The dispatcher told Rachel help was en route. Soon after, sirens blared in the distance. Two cars with flashing lights peeled up the road and into the parking lot. An ambulance screeched to a halt behind them. Lights and shouts filled the air. Men swarmed from the vehicles.

An hour and a half later, Rachel shivered in the front seat of a patrol car and Harry huddled in the backseat, snoring sporadically.

"Sorry to keep you folks waiting so long," Sheriff Victor Garcia said, sliding behind the wheel. He had just finished at the crime scene. Brown-skinned and stocky, he had dark hair, a thick mustache, and eyebrows that, even at five feet, five inches made him seem imposing.

Or was it the uniform? Either way, Rachel had developed a healthy respect for the man. As tired as she was, she recognized that he'd done his job with quick proficiency.

In under an hour he'd moved the birdwatchers away from the crime scene, cordoned off the area with bright yellow police tape, and taken brief statements from everyone present. Then, after surveying the scene, he'd called in the forensic team, members of which were still busy collecting and bagging evidence.

Garcia clipped his seat belt across his lap and cranked the starter. A blast of cold air vented at Rachel's face.

"Oops." He reached over and flipped it off. Rachel forced a smile.

"Thanks."

"No problem," he said, shifting into drive.

Harry stirred in the back seat. "What happens now, Sheriff?"

Garcia glanced in the rearview mirror. "We go to Bird Haven, where you get to answer some more questions."

Harry groaned. "What more can we possibly tell you?"

"That depends on what everyone else has said."

Rachel chewed on Garcia's answer. From the little she knew about police procedure, she assumed that the others had been taken to Bird Haven and requestioned. She was positive Aunt Miriam had skirted the subject of Monday's conversation with Donald Bursau, but what had Gertie coughed up? Rachel hated to speculate.

Bird Haven was lit up like Times Square when they pulled into the driveway. Lights shone from every window, and lanterns lit the walks winding around the main house and the raptor rehabilitation facility.

As Garcia set the parking brake, Rachel climbed out. Harry led the way up the porch steps. The sheriff brought up the rear.

No sooner had they stepped through the door than Perky swooped down on them. Rachel raised her arms in the form of a cross. "Back off, bird."

"What the...?" Garcia's hand dropped to his gun.

Rachel considered letting him draw.

"He's Aunt Miriam's pet," she finally said, cringing as the bird ripped out a strand of her hair and flew away. "Seems he has a thing for red."

The sheriff smoothed his mustache, wiping away a smile. "If I were you, Mrs. Stanhope, I'd consider dyeing my hair."

"I'll take it under advisement."

The sheriff's men had gathered the birdwatchers in the living room. Miriam and Charles sat together on the couch, his arm draped protectively across its back and his hand resting lightly on her shoulder. Dorothy and Cecilia perched on the hearth. Gertie had settled in an armchair, and Forest and Eric sat at a table near the window, engaged in a game of chess.

Harry joined the men at the chess table. Rachel plopped down next to Aunt Miriam and considered knocking Charles's hand away.

Signaling to one of his men, the sheriff leafed through a stack of papers the officer handed to him, then smiled. "Okay, folks. Looks like we have everything we need."

"Does that mean we can go?" Forest asked.

"There's just one more thing. I'd appreciate it if you didn't talk about the case with anyone." He glanced around, waiting for signs of cooperation, then pointed to a gangly deputy with a clipboard. "You all know Deputy Brill. He's going to be handing out business cards with both my home and office numbers on them. If you remember anything, anything at all, call me."

The group nodded, then stood in unison like boot camp recruits being dismissed for the first time. Several of them murmured good-byes, Lark tossed Rachel a wave, and Charles pecked Miriam's cheek. Gertie stopped at the door and drew the sheriff aside.

"I wish I was a knot in the wall so I could hear what she's telling him," Rachel whispered to Miriam. She would lay odds it had something to do with Bursau's quick checkout on Monday afternoon. Deputy Brill shot Rachel a dirty look, and gestured for her to move to a different chair.

Harry was almost out the door when the sheriff intercepted him. "I still have a few questions for you, if you don't mind. In here." Garcia gestured toward the kitchen. "And I'd appreciate it if you'd wait here in the living room, Mrs. Stanhope."

A dejected-looking Harry followed the sheriff into the kitchen, and Rachel slumped into the seat Gertie had vacated. After a moment, Miriam rose.

"If you don't mind, dear, I think I'll go up to bed." She looked exhausted, with dark circles under her eyes, her pale skin wrinkled with worry.

"That's a good idea, Aunt Miriam. It looks like this may take a while."

"You can wake me when you're finished, if you like."

"Let's see how it goes. If you're sleeping, we can talk in the morning."

Miriam nodded, her eyes closed. Though middle-aged, tonight she looked old.

"Good night, dear."

"Good night, Aunt Miriam."

Two magazines and a cup of coffee later, Rachel looked up as Harry bolted from the kitchen. He flashed Rachel a thumbs-up, then scampered for the door.

Deputy Brill escorted Rachel to where Garcia was ensconced in the breakfast nook. A cozy cranny built into an oversized bay window, it consisted of a small table flanked by built-in benches. Green-and-white checked curtains draped the windows, and matching material covered the thick foam cushions that softened the seats. Rachel slid onto the unoccupied bench.

"So, we meet again."

"Tell me, Mrs. Stanhope," Garcia said without preamble, "exactly what happened out there tonight?"

She met his gaze squarely. "Call me Rachel. And how many times are you going to make me repeat the story? We've gone over and over this. Everything's in my statement."

"I'd like to hear it again, if you don't mind."

Obviously the sheriff was fishing for something. "Maybe it would be easier if you just tell me what you want to hear."

Garcia smiled patiently, crossed his arms, and leaned back against the bench.

Rachel gave up on the idea of soaking her bones warm in the hot tub, and repeated the events leading up to the discovery of the body. "We were all at The Thicket looking for this little bird called a LeConte's sparrow. It likes grass, and shouldn't be here, but someone spotted one on Monday afternoon."

"I'm with you so far."

"I heard something hiss, then a lot of crackling in the bushes. More than one little bird could make." A shiver shimmied along her spine. Had it been the killer she'd heard?

Garcia replied as though reading her thoughts. "He's been dead for a while."

Rachel drew a breath. "I decided to go find the others. I ran into Lark first, and she asked me to point out where I'd heard the hissing. We were pishing..."

"I know the term."

"...when I snagged my socks on a log, bent down, and touched the body. I screamed for Lark, and everyone started showing up. Once Eric arrived, he took charge and had me call 911."

"Did everyone seem surprised that you'd found a body?"

"Of course!"

"No one acted strangely?"

Rachel considered how to answer the question. Aunt Miriam had been horrified, Charles had done what men do: he'd taken charge of Miriam.

Harry had checked the victim's pulse, taken initial control, and passed the reins off to Eric when he'd arrived with Forest, who had asked the obvious question: Why would someone want to kill Bursau?

Gertie seemed more upset over the fact it was Bursau who died than over the fact someone was murdered.

And Dorothy'd been horrified that Cecilia's main concern was the restriction on birding The Thicket.

"Everyone was upset," Rachel finally said.

Garcia nodded. "What about the vibes among the group? Any tensions? Any trouble?"

"Such as?" Rachel shifted in her chair. She gazed at the moon perched high in the sky above the silhouette of the Raptor House. She knew he was asking about the confrontation between Gertie and Aunt Miriam. She wondered just how much the others had told him.

Garcia leaned forward. "I say we put all the cards on the table. I know that Gertie said Miriam was one of the last people to see this guy alive." He paused. "I also know that your aunt and the victim had a meeting in the barn on Monday afternoon."

Rachel dropped her gaze to her hands. It was common knowledge that the reporter had been out to see Miriam. The question was, how much had Aunt Miriam told the sheriff about their discussion?

"Gertie told us that Bursau checked out of his motel after his visit to the Raptor House on Monday," Rachel said. "This is Thursday. Has the man been dead for three days?"

The sheriff's eyes narrowed. "I'm asking the questions."

She had struck a nerve. It suddenly occurred to Rachel that maybe she, and/or Aunt Miriam, needed a lawyer.

"Now I'll repeat the question. What happened during the meeting in the barn? Lark says you arrived here on Monday afternoon, about quarter past four. You talked with her for a few minutes, then went outside to find your aunt. Shortly after that, Lark witnessed the victim stomp out of the barn, get in his car, and drive away."

Rachel wet her lips. Should she tell him about the warning or not? Not. "Bursau was on his way out when I arrived. My aunt introduced us. Then he left."

"They weren't arguing?" Garcia asked, stroking his mustache. He knitted his brow until it looked like he had one dark eyebrow slashing the width of his forehead. "The guy wasn't angry about something?"

Aware that she was a horrible liar, Rachel glanced away. "I don't know."

"Rachel, you're only making it worse. I'm not sure what you're covering up or who you're protecting, but my gut says you're hiding something." He sat back and massaged his neck, pinching the skin into tiny rolls of fat. "I've known your aunt a long time. I think she's hiding something, too."

"To what purpose?"

"Somebody contacted that man and lured him to his death. I don't want to believe it was Miriam, but I have to get at the truth. A man is dead."

Either Garcia wanted her to know that the man had been dead since Monday, or he had inadvertently let it slip. Either way, Gertie'd been on to something. "The truth is, Sheriff, I came in on the tail end of the discussion. I'm really not sure what the reporter wanted to know."

Rachel read disbelief in his eyes, but Garcia dropped the subject. "Okay, then let's get back to you," he said. "What brought you here for the summer?"

Rachel tensed. "I don't see how that's relevant."

"Humor me."

Why not? Especially if it steered the conversation away from Aunt Miriam. "I've been having some trouble with my marriage."

"What kind of trouble?"

Rachel pulled herself up straight. "That is definitely none of your business, and definitely not related to anything that's happened since I arrived here."

"Why don't you let me be the judge of that?"

There was no logical reason Sheriff Garcia needed to know anything about her relationship with Roger. "I don't care to talk about this."

"Things must have been bad to drive you away," he said. His dark gaze held steady on her face.

She blinked, forcing back the tears. "If you have to know, I'm getting divorced, all right? Aunt Miriam thought I could use a break, and offered to let me stay here while she's away. End of story."

Garcia looked contrite, then shrugged. "Where's Miriam going?"

Rachel swallowed. Surely Aunt Miriam had told him she was leaving. "On a birding tour."

"Where?"

"Why not ask her?"

"I did. Now I'm asking you."

"She's going to the Middle East."

"Do you know where?"

"Look, Sheriff, I'm not Aunt Miriam's travel agent. Maybe you should ask her for a copy of the itinerary."

"I did." He smiled, then stroked his mustache again. "I hear you're some hotshot public relations person."

"So they tell me."

"Ever do any freelance work?"

Rachel frowned, unable to reconcile his line of questioning. "Why?"

"I'm involved with a youth camp up here. We could use a brochure and some help putting together a fund-raising campaign. It's pro bono work. Do you think you might be interested?"

The request came out of left field, but he'd piqued her curiosity. "What kind of 'youth'?"

"Troubled." He scooted out of the breakfast nook. "Like I said, it's all pro bono. Give it some thought."

"I'll do that." She'd never done any freebie work, but if the cause was good...

"Great." He flashed a smile, then added, "I hope I don't need to tell you not to leave town."

A line right out of a TV cop show, and here she'd started to think maybe there was more to this man than the stereotype. "I'll let you know if I plan to go anywhere."

"Good." He started to walk away, then swiveled back. "Oh, by the way, that goes for Miriam, too."

Chapter 6

Rachel charged upstairs to Aunt Miriam's room the minute she'd closed the door behind Garcia. Her aunt had a few questions to answer now that Bursau was dead. Like had she had any further contact with the man before his murder? And just how serious did she think his warning was?

Dappled moonlight illuminated the master suite. A short hallway led past a walk-in closet, a bathroom, and into an oversized room furnished with a bed, two nightstands, two dressers, and a loveseat. A half-packed suitcase was open on the floor near the foot of the bed. Aunt Miriam lay snuggled under the covers, her hair braided and wrapped around her head like a halo, a light snore seesawing past her lips.

The urge to shake her awake tingled in Rachel's fingers, but, in the end, she clenched her hands and went to bed without waking Miriam.

Morning came early after a fitful night's rest, and Rachel made a beeline for Miriam's bedroom. She found the bed made and her aunt gone. A sweep of the house turned up only Perky. In fact, the only sign that anyone besides Rachel had been there was the half-full pot of freshly brewed coffee on the kitchen countertop.

Had Miriam gone to the Raptor House?

Rachel poured herself a mug of coffee and mulled over the events of the previous evening. Two things were clear. Donald Bursau was dead, and Sheriff Garcia believed one of the birdwatchers was the killer. But which one? She didn't know much about any of them. And when had the murder actually occurred?

Monday, after Eric's announcement about the spotting of the LeConte's sparrow, the entire group had rushed down to scour The Thicket. All in all, counting the others already there, there must have been more than twenty people.

Outside, a bird screeched. Rachel stepped to the window. A flock of ravens wheeled into the meadow stretching from the back door to the mountains. In the distance, the tangle of willows, white alder, and weeds wound along Black Canyon Creek, kissed golden by the morning sun. The Thicket. In this light, it hardly looked like a place for a murder.

Farther out, Long's Peak rose 14,000 feet, towering above the snowcapped mountains of the Continental Divide. The range scalloped the blue horizon until the peaks disappeared behind the Raptor House and Lumpy Ridge. God's country, or the Devil's playground?

Rachel refilled her mug, and slipped out the back door to see if Aunt Miriam had gone to talk with Eric. A Norwegian transplant with a veterinary degree, he stopped by early in the mornings to clean the cages and care for the birds, then returned every afternoon.

The barn was empty except for Isaac. The eagle flapped his wing when Rachel entered. She sidled past, her loafers kicking up dust that shimmered in the light filtering through the cracks in the shutters. Spiderwebs clung to the rafters in clumps.

She found Eric in the back room, stuffing dead birds into the microwave. "Good morning," she said.

He glanced up from across a table covered in brown-feathered bodies. Distaste must have shown on her face, because he grinned, holding up a carcass by one leg. "Coturnix quail. The falcons love 'em."

"Yum," she said, hugging the doorway. "Have you seen Aunt Miriam?"

"Ja, she stopped in before leaving. She went birding with Charles at Barr Lake."

"Where's that?"

"A couple of hours southeast of here. I doubt they'll be back before dinner."

So much for waiting until morning. Rachel edged closer. "What are you doing?"

"Thawing bird food."

"Do you do this everyday?"

He shook his head. "Normally we transfer the dead birds from the freezer to the refrigerator, or leave them out overnight. But with all the excitement…" He pressed a knife blade against the quail flesh. "It needs just another minute or two."

Her gaze took in the three-tiered metal rack of dead birds pushed in front of the large walk-in freezer. Curiosity overrode her squeamishness. "Do you buy all these frozen?"

"No." He punched the Quick Minute button on the microwave. "We raise them in the chicken coop. It provides a steady supply, which is good because it takes a lot of meat to feed all the birds we're housing in here." The timer dinged. He opened the microwave and knifed the quail. "Ah, good. It's done."

It looked inedible. "Do you come in every day?"

"Ja, mostly." He scooped the thawed quail into two large buckets. "I try and take one day off a week. It changes, based on when Miriam or some other EPOCH member can cover for me. I'll admit, it's hard for me to leave this job alone." He shouldered the back door open. "Would you like a tour?"

"I'd love one." Rachel followed him along the narrow pathway. A fly buzzed back and forth between the open buckets, lured by the smell of dead flesh and blood. All she'd seen of the facility was the barn and Collegiate Hall. Since then, the days had been consumed by work, the search for the LeConte's sparrow, and now a murder investigation. "Do you mind if I ask you a question?"

Eric signaled a turn toward the Protective Custody House. The hospital wing, if she remembered right. "Shoot," he said.

"Did Donald Bursau contact you about his story before he died?"

Eric's step faltered. "No, he didn't."

"He never left you any message, or made any contact?" She stood to the side, holding open the door of the building, allowing Eric to enter. His face was emotionless.

"No. In fact, I'd never even heard of him before you found his body."

That seemed odd. Especially if Bursau was the reporter Gertie claimed he was.

Eric changed the subject, identifying the birds inside the cages. He fed quail to twelve red-tailed hawks, three peregrine falcons, and a golden eagle. He tossed dead mice to the

American kestrels and owls.

Freedom House was the last stop on their itinerary.

"We have a white gyrfalcon in here," he said. "Some kid found her in a pasture near Loveland. Her wing was broken, but it's healing well. She's almost ready for release."

Rachel peered through the observation slit. A large white bird with feathered pantaloons and black hash marks on its back and wings perched on a tree limb. The bucket clanged against the door when Eric entered the cage, and the bird swiveled its head. Wide-set dark eyes stared calmly in their direction.

Rachel stared back. "It's beautiful. I've never seen a bird like that."

"We don't see many gyrfalcons in the United States, especially not whites."

"Why's that?"

"They're arctic breeders. They live in Greenland and Alaska, way north. When the winter's hard, some of the grays migrate south, but even I'd never seen a white gyr in the wild before."

"How do you think it ended up here?"

"She may have been blown off course by a storm, or..." He shrugged.

"Or what?"

"Personally, I think she belonged to a falconer, though we did some checking around and no one's claimed her. She wasn't wearing a metal band, but still..." Eric locked the door to the gyrfalcon's cage and led Rachel out the back door to a fenced-in chicken coop. A brood of quail skittered away as Eric undid the gate. "Falconers are required to band their birds."

Rachel envisioned an adjustable band, like the self-sizing rings delivered in gumball machines. Those eventually broke apart. "Maybe it fell off?"

"No way. Birds bred in captivity are fitted with seamless bands. They're put on while the chicks are small. There's no way to get one off without cutting it or tearing off the bird's leg. The wild birds wear aluminum bands crimped around tight with metal pliers." He circled his thumb and middle finger, pinching them together. "If the bird lost a band, her leg would likely be marked in some way. This gyr's perfect, now that her wing is healed."

"Then what makes you think she belonged to someone?"

"For one thing, I've never seen a white gyrfalcon this far south. We see maybe half a dozen gyrfalcon total in Colorado. Mostly during December, January, and February. All of them gray. This white was found in March. Very late."

Eric captured a young quail and carried it back to Freedom House, releasing it into the cage with the gyrfalcon. The quail scurried into the vegetation.

"Don't tell me," Rachel said. "She eats the bird?"

"We need to know she can hunt before we can release her."

The quail darted toward the perimeter of the cage, searching for better cover.

"The poor thing."

"The gyr has to eat."

The grass rustled, and Rachel could no longer spot the quail.

"If the falcon belonged to someone around here and you release her, will she go home?" she asked.

"No. Falcons are lost all the time. The best we can hope is that she uses her natural instincts to migrate north. Hopefully, she can assimilate back to the wild. She'll be banded and outfitted with a transmitter. If she hangs around too long, I'll go out and pick her up. Then we'll have to winter her over and release her the next time another gyrfalcon is spotted in the area."

"Hoping that she follows it?"

"You've got the picture."

The large white bird swiveled its neck, then rose in the air with slow, steady wing beats. It must have spotted the quail.

"She's very majestic-looking," Rachel said.

"Ja. In the olden days, only a king could fly the gyrfalcon. That's why falconry is called the 'sport of kings.'"

Rachel had assumed it was an activity that had gone out with the Dark Ages. "How many falconers are there? I mean, there aren't many kings left in this world."

"I'd say the North American Falconry Association has twenty-five hundred to three thousand members. Plus there are groups all over the world. The Arabs love flying the birds."

Aunt Miriam's explanation of Bursau's questions played

through her mind. He'd asked her about falcons disappearing from the Raptor House.

"Where do they get their birds? Can they come here and get one?"

"No. Falconers are permitted to cull a certain number of birds from the wild, if they obtain the proper permits. But a raptor rehabilitation center like this one is dedicated to saving birds for release, not for hunting or propagation."

"What about endangered species? Can those be taken from the wild?"

"Certain birds are not allowed. All falcons are protected by the Migratory Bird Treaty Act, plus the Convention on International Trade in Endangered Species and the Lacey Act Amendments. The Lacey Act makes it illegal to transport, sell, or acquire birds in violation of state, federal, or foreign law. Which essentially means that certain species are off-limits. The penalties for violation are very stiff."

"So do the majority of falconers buy their birds?"

"Ja, but there are only a handful of licensed breeders in the Rocky Mountain area. Very few falconers are granted propagation licenses."

Rachel watched the white gyrfalcon soar the length of the cage. "What does a bird like this cost?"

"From a breeder? Upwards of five thousand to eight thousand dollars. An overseas buyer would pay a lot more. A white gyrfalcon like this one would bring close to a hundred thousand dollars. That's if you could get her out of the U.S."

Rachel turned away from the cage as the gyrfalcon dived. She heard the frantic rustle of grasses, a sharp whistle, then a crunching of bones. A meal fit for a queen.

Rachel spent the rest of the afternoon working. With the computer setup from Images Plus, and no interruptions from coworkers or clients, she was able to accomplish in five hours what normally took eight. Today's project had been constructing a web page for a Massachusetts-based writer whose book, Market Yourself a Bestseller, hit number 15 on the Publisher's Weekly list. When it remained there only one week, the writer had sought professional help.

She e-mailed her file to the office, clicked to go offline, then changed her mind. Maybe there was something about Donald Bursau or his story on the Internet.

She typed in "Birds of a Feather magazine," and clicked GO. An interactive web page appeared on screen. Feature Stories popped up in a flush of ducks. The only recent article by Donald Bursau was on America's disappearing wetlands, so Rachel clicked back to the home page. About Our Writers produced better results. A full set of writer bios appeared. Donald Bursau's name was first on the list.

Born in New Jersey, Bursau had moved to Montana after graduating from the University of Colorado's School of Journalism in 1978. An animal rights activist, he had sat in, marched, and protested every form of animal abuse known to man. In 1986 he won a prestigious award for his story on Operation Falcon, a sting conducted by the U.S. Fish and Wildlife Service to crack down on the illegal trade in wild birds of prey.

It took her a few minutes, but Rachel finally found the story buried in the magazine's archives. Published in 1985, it detailed a three-year undercover operation involving a hundred and fifty Fish and Wildlife Service special agents, and an equal number of state wildlife officers. Arrest warrants had been issued, and sixty-three persons had been charged with illegal trafficking in what was classified as a "multi-million dollar smuggling industry," providing wild birds to overseas falconries.

The article went on to list a number of the defendants, many charged with laundering birds through legitimate breeding operations. It ended with a reference to a "key player from Colorado" who had slipped through the cracks.

Uncle William? That was around the time he and Aunt Miriam had purchased the ranch and started the rehab center.

In the 1970s, William had conducted research studies to determine the long-term effects of DDT on peregrine falcons. A decline in the species population had caused the bird to be placed on the endangered list. Studies showed that an accumulation of the pesticide caused aberrant breeding behavior and thin-shelled eggs, reducing hatching success.

William's analyses had required the collection of unhatched eggs. Was he also gathering viable eggs and selling them on the black market? The thought seemed ludicrous. Why take the risk? Unless Aunt Miriam was wrong about his pension, and he'd needed the money to help finance the purchase of Bird Haven. She made a note to look into Uncle William's past financial situation.

A search for information on "Operation Falcon" resulted in only a few short citations that recapped the information in Bursau's article, so Rachel clicked back to the Birds of a Feather home page and jotted down the telephone number. An additional search of the online White Pages provided a Montana phone number and street address for the deceased reporter.

She dialed the magazine offices first. A crisp voice came through the line. "Birds of a Feather. May I help you?"

Rachel decided to take the direct approach. "I need some information on Donald Bursau, please."

"One moment."

Muzak featuring the songbirds of the Americas blasted in Rachel's ear, then a man's voice. "Who is this?"

Her response was automatic. "Rachel Stanhope. I have a few questions regarding Donald Bursau."

"Mr. Bursau is unavailable."

That's an understatement. "I'm interested in getting some information on a story he was working."

Silence followed, then a rustling of paper. "Who are you? Are you a reporter?"

"No, I'm just…" What? The woman who found his body? Rachel decided to try a different tack. "I spoke with him Monday afternoon, and wanted to clarify some information he gave me."

"I'm afraid I can't help you."

"Then who can?" She tapped her pencil point against the yellow legal pad on the table and remembered the sign posted in Jack Jaffery's office. Go Straight to the Top. "Is the editor in chief available?"

There was another silence, and this time she feared the man

had hung up.

"He's not. Now unless you have something else..." The question dangled, and Rachel heard more rustling of papers.

"Who are you?" she demanded, hoping he'd realize she wasn't going to drop the matter.

"The name's Kirk Udall. I've been assigned to cover Bursau's beat for awhile. He's, ah, a little out of commission right now."

"Mr. Udall, I know Bursau's dead." Rachel debated whether or not she should tell him some of the other things she knew. "I also know his story had some connection to my Uncle William."

"Tanager? William Tanager?"

There was unchecked interest in his voice. "Yes."

"You've got my full attention."

"The afternoon before he died, Donald Bursau came out to see my aunt. He warned her to be cautious around some of William's colleagues. She and I dismissed the idea as crazy, but now that Bursau's dead, I'm concerned my aunt may be in danger."

"And...?"

"I'd like to know what he knew."

Udall laughed. "Well, we can't very well ask him, can we?" He paused. "Besides, what possible motive would I have for sharing information with you?"

"A clear conscience."

"Have you talked about this with your aunt?"

I tried. "She claims she doesn't know anything."

The clock ticked while she waited for his reply. "You know, Ms. Stanhope, I have competitors at Birder's World and Birding just dying to scoop me on this story. If you'd consider cutting a deal and selling me an exclusive to your story, maybe I could scrounge up something that would help you." He coughed. "You know, you scratch my back and I'll scratch yours."

Rachel checked her temper by doodling on the pad. "How about this, Mr. Udall? You tell me what you know, and I'll tell you if there's any basis in fact."

He laughed again, harder this time. "Right, like I'm going to trust you."

Rachel bristled. "What makes you so sure Bursau had

everything right?"

"What makes you so sure he didn't?"

She didn't have a good reply, and since it was clear she wasn't getting anywhere, she hung up and dialed Bursau's home number. Maybe he had a wife or girlfriend who would answer the phone. Instead his voicemail picked up. Rachel didn't leave a message.

By then it was five o'clock, and her appetite, which had flown the coop in the Raptor House that morning, had returned with a vengeance. Deciding a toasted cheese sandwich sounded good, Rachel shut down the computer and headed for the kitchen.

The house, drenched in the long afternoon shadows, seemed lonely. Besides herself, Perky was the only one home. Rachel wished Aunt Miriam would get back.

She was contemplating calling out a posse when Lark and Eric banged in through the back door.

"Hey, Rae. Where's Miriam?" Lark asked. She wheezed the words out, her face flushed.

Up until the past few days, Rae had been a nickname used exclusively by Miriam. When had that changed? "She's not back yet."

"Are you sure?" Eric dropped into a chair, rubbing his hands over his reddened face.

"You were the one who told me she went to Barr Lake and wouldn't be back before dinner. I haven't seen her all day."

Lark slammed her hand down on the granite breakfast bar.

Rachel glanced from one to the other. "What is it? What's wrong?"

"You're positive she's not here?" urged Lark.

"One hundred percent. Now, will one of you please tell me what's going on?"

"The peregrines are missing," Lark said.

Eric looked up. "So's the white gyrfalcon."

"Missing?" Rachel wet her lips. "I don't understand."

"What's there to understand?" Lark said. "It's simple. The birds are gone."

Chapter 7

Rachel figured there had to be a logical explanation for the birds' disappearance. "Maybe somebody moved them to a different cage."

"We thought of that," Lark replied. "We checked."

"Well, maybe someone moved them to a different facility," Rachel suggested. "Isn't there another rehab center near Boulder?"

"Ja," Eric said. "But I called the main office. No one with the Park Service has been out here today, except for me."

"And I checked with all the EPOCH member volunteers," Lark added. She pulled a pitcher of iced tea out of the refrigerator, then rummaged in the cupboard. "Same thing."

Eric raked a hand through his hair. "It makes no sense that they're gone."

"Maybe they escaped," Rachel said.

"Not a chance." Lark poured tea into a tall glass, then held up the pitcher. "Anyone else?"

Eric and Rachel both shook their heads. Eric walked to the patio doors and stared out toward the Raptor House. "The cages were locked up tight, but even if the doors had been opened, only the gyr might fly. The peregrines haven't fledged yet."

"So what you're saying is someone stole them?"

"That's how it looks," Lark said, pressing her glass against the ice dispenser in the refrigerator door. Cubes clinked into the iced tea.

"What about security? Isn't there some sort of system in place?"

Eric shook his head. "We've never needed one."

"The Park Service has keys to the cages," explained Lark, "and there's a set in the office for the volunteers. Anyone could have picked them up. It's never been a problem."

"The question is, why would anyone take them?" Eric asked. "Those birds have no value to anyone."

Lark took a swig of her drink, then plunked the glass down on the breakfast nook table. "That's not exactly true. The gyrfalcon's worth a bundle, given the right buyer."

Eric frowned, turning away from the door. "Get real, Lark. If someone planned to make any money, they'd need a foreign buyer. And a way to smuggle the gyr out of the country. There's no way. Not after the crackdown following Operation Falcon."

"What about the peregrines?" Rachel asked.

Eric slapped nonexistent dirt from his jeans. "Their value's even more limited. Someone in need of new stock might want them for propagation. But why they take the chance of stealing wild birds when you can purchase a captive-bred bird from an authorized breeder for between six hundred and fifteen hundred dollars. The penalties for misappropriating wildlife are just too stiff to take those risks."

Lark took another swig of her tea, prompting Rachel to change her mind. Pouring herself a glass, she asked, "Just how stiff are they?"

Eric straddled a kitchen stool, leaned on the counter, and raised a finger. "For one violation of the Lacey Act, a person's looking at a five-year prison term and up to twenty thousand dollars in fines."

"Multiply that by three," Lark added. "Hey"—she snapped her fingers—"what if somebody's trying to discredit Miriam or the Raptor House?"

"Why would anyone want to do that?" Eric asked.

Rachel could venture a guess. She recalled Donald Bursau's warning to Miriam, and began to suspect that the birds' disappearance had something to do with his death. One thing she knew for sure: Aunt Miriam was going to flip when she learned the falcons were gone. "I think we should call the sheriff."

"I already did," Eric said.

Lark carried her tea into the family room. Setting it down on the fireplace mantel, she stared out the window. "Rae, are you sure Miriam hasn't been home?"

"Positive. Why do you keep asking me that?"

"Because her car's parked outside."

Rachel crossed the family room and peered out the window.

Sure enough, Miriam's green Toyota was angled into a space near the front of the house. "She must have ridden with Charles."

Lark fingered her thick braid. "Of course."

Then another possibility struck Rachel, sending fear sluicing through her. "Unless...what if she came home and surprised someone taking the birds?"

Lark's fingers froze in position. "Don't even say that."

"But what if—"

"I told you not to say that."

Eric pulled up straight. "That's a crazy idea."

Rachel hoped she was wrong. "Look at the chain of events. Donald Bursau comes out to talk with Miriam, warns her to be careful, and then—"

"He did what?" Lark interrupted.

"He told her to watch her back. Three days later, you and I found his body in The Thicket, and, according to Gertie, he disappeared sometime Monday."

"Ja, but who can believe anything Gertie says?" Eric asked.

Rachel shrugged. "Sheriff Garcia agreed. And now, the birds are missing."

"There's still no reason to jump to conclusions," Eric protested. "For all we know, Miriam is still with Charles. Or, if she did come home, maybe she took the birds...somewhere?"

"Like where?" Lark asked, turning away from the window. "Where would she take them?"

"And why?" Rachel asked.

Eric grimaced and scratched his head. "You're right. I'm reaching."

Lark picked up her glass and studied it, twisting it in a ray of sunlight and sparking a shower of rainbows. "I don't know. It's possible she might have taken them if she thought they were in danger."

"But why would they be in danger?" said a voice from the doorway.

Rachel whirled, surprised to find Sheriff Garcia leaning against the dining room door jamb. "How long have you been here?"

"Long enough to hear the tail end of your conversation," he said, stepping into the room. "Your aunt didn't tell you where she was going this morning?"

"She told Eric," Rachel replied. "She and Charles went birding at Barr Lake."

Garcia glanced at Eric. "Is that true?"

"That's what she said," Eric replied. Then, as if it was an afterthought, he added, "I'm sure they're still there."

Rachel's twinge of fear grew to a stab. "What time did you tell me they'd be home?"

"Around dinnertime, but I was only guessing."

Sheriff Garcia stroked his mustache. "Okay, let's work another problem. What time did you notice the birds missing?"

"A little after five o'clock," replied Eric.

"Any signs of a break-in?"

"None."

"Which means that someone used a key to gain access to the birds."

"Ja. It looks like."

Rachel's stab of fear had now grown to a gash. "Sheriff, what if my aunt surprised the birdnapper? She may have been kidnapped, or…"

"We'll find her," he said calmly, fixing Rachel with a steady gaze. "It's like when one of my kids disappears from the shelter. They may run, but they always leave behind a clue."

Suddenly Lark, who had remained silent until then, drew herself up. "Are you saying you think Miriam took off with the birds?"

Garcia studied her, rubbing his fingers back and forth along his jaw. "Now that you mention it, the possibility crossed my mind."

The two faced off. Eric scowled from his seat at the kitchen counter. Finally Rachel stepped between them. "Look, this is getting us nowhere."

"She's right," Eric said.

Garcia was first to break off the stare. His gaze flitted around the room. "I think the first thing I need to do is take a look around. Unless, of course, you have any objections."

"None." Rachel prayed Aunt Miriam didn't have any secrets to hide. "Be my guest."

Together the four of them scoured the premises. Other than the two empty cages, the Raptor House teemed with life. Birds screeched and squawked. Wings battered the air.

Perky made his requisite appearance during their sweep of Bird Haven, dive-bombing Rachel as she stood at the end of Miriam's bed. Otherwise, nothing seemed disturbed.

"Okay, there's no sign of a struggle, no sign of forced entry," Garcia said, once they were back in the kitchen. "So what did we learn?"

"That it's an inside job," Eric concluded.

Garcia nodded his head in agreement. "Who all was here on Monday?"

"Why?" Rachel asked, already sure of the answer.

"Because I checked the records on the telephone call Donald Bursau received just before checking out of his hotel. That call came from here."

"From Bird Haven?" Rachel, Lark, and Eric exclaimed in unison.

Garcia nodded. "Someone placed the call from a phone on the premises around six o'clock."

"We were all here, along with half a dozen other EPOCH members. Eric arrived with the news that a LeConte's sparrow was spotted about quarter to six."

"Ja. Harry drove me up from The Thicket, then left right away."

"Did he make a phone call?" Garcia asked.

"I don't think so."

"Look," Lark said, "none of us had anything to do with that man's murder. So if you're suggesting that one of us lured Donald Bursau to his death, Vic, you're barking up the wrong tree."

"The evidence speaks for itself," declared Garcia, punctuating the statement with sharp jabs against the countertop. "It's a fact. Someone called Bursau from this house on Monday evening." He paused, tipping his head as though testing the weight of his next statement. "Plus, the coroner places his death on Monday, between seven o'clock and midnight. You do the math."

Rachel didn't believe what she was hearing. Was it possible that one of the birdwatchers was behind Bursau's murder? There were phones all over the house. There was even one in the bathroom. Any one of them could have made the phone call. So who else had been here that night, aside from the three of them and Aunt Miriam? Dorothy MacBean and Cecilia Meyer. Andrew and Opal Henderson. Forest Nettleman, Charles Pendergast, and Gertie.

"Rachel, are you absolutely positive your aunt's not been back today?" Garcia asked, picking up a framed photograph of Miriam and Will taken at the entrance to Rocky Mountain National Park.

"One hundred percent," she answered, pushing aside the nagging doubts that had plagued her since the trip to look around upstairs. She hadn't realized it until now, but Miriam's suitcase, the one she'd been packing for her trip to the Middle East, was gone.

It had been on the floor at the end of the bed, where Rachel stood while Garcia and the others conducted their sweep of the master suite. It had been there this morning. It had been there for days. For it to disappear two weeks prior to Miriam's scheduled departure for the Middle East, a place with more active falconers per capita than any other region—not to mention falconers who'd been known to spend exorbitant sums to acquire prized birds—seemed too coincidental. Rachel feared the conclusions Garcia might draw and was unsure what to think herself.

Footsteps at the door saved her from further thought. Charles Pendergast strode into the kitchen, decked out in full birder garb—tan pants, tan shirt, and an olive-green vest with pencils, pens, and pads sticking out of the multiple pockets. "Where's Miriam?" he asked.

"We thought she was with you," Lark declared.

"Ja," agreed Eric. "Didn't you and she go birding together?"

"Yes, but I dropped her back here about four o'clock. She wanted to talk with Rachel." Charles shuffled across the floor, his knee-high green waders squeaking against the tile floor like markers on a dry board. He plopped down at the breakfast nook table. "I was supposed to meet her back here around six o'clock. Why? What's up?"

"She seems to be missing," Garcia replied.

"And three of the birds are gone, too," added Eric.

"Is this some sort of joke?" Pendergast's eyes darted from one to the other.

Garcia shook his head. "Sorry, Charles. Tell me, what did she want to talk to Rachel about?"

Charles dropped his gaze to the table. "I don't think I should say. Not if Miriam hasn't spoken with her yet. It's sort of a personal matter."

Garcia placed a hand on his shoulder. "I need you to answer the question."

Rachel saw Lark and Eric exchange glances. The sheriff was watching Charles closely. He ran the toe of his boot across a grouted seam, then raised his head, pinning Rachel with an ice-blue stare. "Miriam wanted to tell Rachel about us. We've been seeing each other for the past year, and things have gotten kind of serious." He cleared his throat. "Miriam and I are in love, Rachel. She wanted to tell you herself. We hope you'll be happy for us."

Lark gasped. "You're getting married?"

"No." Charles toyed with the signet ring on his perfectly manicured hand. "We plan to live together. It was Miriam's idea."

Garcia coughed. Rachel wondered if he was choking on the information, as she was.

Eric congratulated Charles, giving Rachel time to rein in her astonishment. She could tell from the first that Charles was interested in her aunt, but Miriam had never indicated that his interest was reciprocated. At least not to the extent that she would cohabit with the man. Besides, Aunt Miriam had been married three times. She wasn't the live-together type.

"I guess I'll have to take your word for it, until we find Aunt Miriam," Rachel said. She turned to face Garcia. "Can I file a missing-person's report, Sheriff?"

He shook his head. "There's nothing I can do for forty-eight hours."

"Miriam could be dead by then," Lark protested.

"Don't even say that." Rachel moved to the patio doors and pressed her nose to the glass. The warmth of the day lay shrouded in twilight. Long's Peak towered above the valley, a black silhouette against a slate blue sky joined by a rippled line of purple to the craggy outline of Lumpy Ridge. In the distance, The Thicket stretched like a dark fence along the banks of Black Canyon Creek. Rachel flipped on the lights and turned back to Garcia. "What if she's right? What if my aunt is in danger?"

"The best I can do is put out an all-points bulletin in connection with the missing birds," he said, running a hand through his hair. "But, to be honest, the longer I stand around here, the more convinced I am Miriam took those birds herself."

Charles stared slack-mouthed at Garcia. "Have you lost your marbles, Vic?"

"Maybe. But, just to be on the safe side, I think I'll have a few of my guys check out the airport, car rental firms, and the airport and local hotels."

"How many hotels are there?" asked Rachel.

"Locally, around a hundred and seventy-five. That's counting the condominium complexes and the ranching operations."

Rachel's eyes widened. "Are you serious?"

"Hey, last summer Elk Park had over three million visitors," Lark said. "People have to sleep somewhere."

"Added to Denver's airport hotels, you're up to checking about two hundred, then. What are we supposed to do, Sheriff?" Rachel's voice rose, along with her blood pressure. "Sit around here and wait until you find Aunt Miriam's body dumped in The Thicket?"

Shortly thereafter, Garcia had shown himself out. After a few more minutes, Eric headed out to lock up the Raptor House. Charles left right after him, and Lark excused herself to "dig up some writing supplies."

Left alone, stunned by the revelations of the past hour, Rachel sank down on the family room couch and tried to sort everything out.

First, Donald Bursau was dead, and now Miriam was missing, along with three birds from the Raptor House. How were those three things connected? Had one of the birdwatchers been involved in the smuggling scam Bursau was investigating, and killed him to keep things quiet? Had Miriam known who the person was? If so, was she next on the killer's list?

The thought set Rachel's heart racing and her tears flowing. Rachel didn't think she could stand it if anything bad happened to her aunt. Miriam had been like a mother to her the last fourteen years. Perhaps closer, in that she had also been a friend.

Rachel picked up the phone and tried calling her father in Chicago. The answering machine picked up. Rachel didn't leave a message, afraid that Grandma Wilder might intercept it. As she hung up, Lark returned with two legal pads and a couple of pencils.

"Since it's obvious Garcia's going to drag his feet, we'll have to figure this out ourselves," she said, sitting down in the chair opposite Rachel. She scribbled something on her pad, then looked up. Concern flashed across her face. "Are you okay?"

Rachel wiped her eyes with her shirtsleeve. "Yeah, peachy."

Lark reached out and touched her knee. "Hey, Rae, she's okay. Trust me, I feel it."

"I'm okay. I just—" A fresh onslaught of tears robbed her of her voice, and she squeezed her eyes shut to stem the flow. Crying wasn't going to solve anything.

"You've just got to think positive, Rae. Keep a stiff upper lip."

Rachel drew a ragged breath. "You've been hanging around here too much, Lark. You're beginning to sound like her."

"Maybe so, but she'd expect us to do something. Not just sit around and twiddle our thumbs."

Rachel straightened up. Lark had a point. Aunt Miriam wouldn't sit around expecting answers to fall into her lap. She'd dig in like a robin after a worm. "Okay, no twiddling."

"Right, and since it seems like everything ties back to the murder, the first thing I think we should do is figure out which one of us wanted Donald Bursau dead." Lark tapped her pad. "I've listed the suspects, everyone who was here that night. Now let's see if we can figure out any motives."

"You forget something, Lark. I hardly know these people."

"Okay, so I'll go first."

"Great." Rachel forced a smile. "Exercises in futility."

Lark ignored her, placing a checkmark beside the first name on the list. "Dorothy MacBean. She's a spinster. She lives in town with her sister, Cecilia Meyer. Cecilia was married once. She had a three-day honeymoon, then her husband shipped out to Korea and ended up MIA."

"How sad," Rachel said, feeling her tears welling up again.

"Yeah, well, she spends all her time trying to fix Dorothy up. She wants her to experience the thrill of love. Dorothy spends all her time running the opposite way."

"What would be their motives for wanting Bursau dead?"

"Let's see... Dorothy is involved in planning a new wildlife center that's going to be built on the other side of Elk Park, near the entrance to Rocky Mountain National Park. Funding is a little iffy. Money's always a good motive. Plus, she's jealous of Miriam."

"Why?"

"She wants to be president of EPOCH."

"What about Cecilia?"

"She'd kill to protect Dorothy."

"The problem with that theory is the timing. We need a motive that goes back over fifteen years." Rachel realized her mistake instantly, but it was too late to snatch back the words. How could she have let that tidbit of information slip?

Lark's eyes narrowed.

"I guess you have a right to know," Rachel said, before Lark could grill her. "Donald Bursau was asking Aunt Miriam questions about Uncle William's connection to a bird-trafficking scam that took place around 1984."

Lark frowned. "Dorothy and Cecilia have been around that long, but..."

"Let's just keep going." Doing something was making Rachel feel better. "Who's next on the list?"

"The Hendersons. Andrew and Opal. They live in Glen Haven, about ten miles down the canyon. They're fairly new to the area."

"Scratch them, then, unless they have a past we don't know about." Rachel made a mental note to see what she could dig up about them on the Internet.

"Then there's Gertie."

"Well, that's obvious."

"But she would have been only fifteen."

"True, but she'd want to protect Uncle William from scandal, even if he is deceased. If Gertie had an inkling that her father's reputation might be maligned, she'd have killed Bursau in a New York minute."

Lark looked shocked. "So would I."

Rachel eyed her teenage chum, unable to believe her capable of murdering anyone. "Then write it down under motive."

Lark stuck out her tongue. "So what's your motive?"

"I didn't kill him."

"But suppose you had. What would have been your motive?"

Good question. "To protect Aunt Miriam?"

"Why would she need protecting?"

Scooping her hair into a ponytail, Rachel clasped her hands at the back of her head, wishing she could kick herself. "Do you promise to keep this to yourself?"

"Sure."

"Pinky swear?"

Lark tipped her head sideways, then extended her pinky, linking it with Rachel's and giving a shake. "Satisfied?"

"I'm serious. If Sheriff Garcia knew this, it could incriminate Aunt Miriam."

Lark's eyes widened, and she nodded encouragement.

"Bursau implied that Miriam knew about Uncle William's alleged involvement, which would make her an accessory. If he'd printed that in Birds of a Feather, true or not, her reputation would have been ruined."

"I'll add that as motive under me, too." Lark scribbled on the page. "In fact, we could put that as motive under everyone's name."

Rachel slouched back against the couch and lifted her feet to the coffee table. "Who on the list haven't we covered?"

"Forest Nettleman, Eric, Harry, and Charles Pendergast. We

can rule out Harry and Eric."

"Why?"

"We just can."

Fine. Rachel made another mental note to do some checking on the side. "So what about Charles?"

"As you well know, he's an old friend of the family. I suppose it's possible he and William were involved in something together."

Rachel hadn't thought of that possibility. It would be reason enough to kill Bursau, and reason enough to marry Aunt Miriam. Wasn't there a law that spouses didn't have to testify against each other? "Which leaves Forest."

"I don't know about him," Lark said. "He's a congressman, so to him reputation means everything." She frowned suddenly, scratching behind her ear with her pencil eraser. "Though that hasn't kept him clear of Mike Johnson."

"Who?"

"The rancher who owns the adjoining property. He's also a falconer, and has plans for a commercial development that most of Elk Park opposes. Forest seems to think it has some merit, and keeps talking it up around town."

Rachel turned at the sound of the patio door opening. Eric slipped inside, closing the door behind him.

"Charles went home," he announced. "I thought I'd come and see if Miriam had checked in before I took off."

Rachel shook her head.

"What are you two up to?" He gestured toward Lark's legal pad.

"We were compiling a list of suspects in the Donald Bursau murder," Lark declared. "Your name came up."

"Oh, goody."

"Don't worry, we dismissed you as a likely, and were just debating Forest's connection with Mike Johnson as a possible motive."

Eric's face blanched.

"What is it?" asked Rachel, convinced he was about to throw up.

"Mike Johnson was here on Monday."

"What?" Lark said. "What are you talking about?"

"He was down at The Thicket that afternoon. His truck was out of commission, so he caught a ride up here with Harry and me. He came inside, placed a call to the ranch, and had one of his guys pick him up at the end of the road."

Chapter 8

It didn't take long for the three of them to reach the consensus that everyone present at Bird Haven on Monday had a motive to kill Bursau. Except, maybe, the Hendersons. But what about opportunity?

"Sheriff Garcia said Bursau was killed between seven o'clock and midnight," Rachel said. "I stayed here Monday night, but the rest of you were down at The Thicket. Did anyone hear a gunshot?"

Eric glanced at Lark, and they both shook their heads. "Not that I know of," he said. "Heck, there must have been twenty of us down there, possibly more."

"That must mean Bursau bought it after we'd called it a night," Lark said. "I was home by nine."

"Ja, same here."

"Can anyone vouch for either of you?"

Again, they exchanged glances. "No."

Rachel frowned. Miriam had arrived back at the house around nine-thirty, then the two of them had hot chocolate and headed to bed. Even Miriam could have sneaked back without anyone knowing. "So everyone had opportunity."

"Except maybe the Hendersons," Lark said. "They live pretty far down the canyon."

It was after midnight when Eric left. Lark insisted on spending the night. Pulling out the sleeper sofa, the two women settled in like teenagers at a slumber party. Lark made popcorn. Rachel poured colas. And they waited for Aunt Miriam to come in or call. She did neither.

The next morning, Rachel woke to the smell of freshly brewed coffee and fried eggs.

"Rise and shine, sleepy head." Lark deposited a mug of coffee on the end table. "Man, did you zonk out last night."

Rachel sat up, pulling her knees to her chest. She was surprised she'd been able to sleep a wink. "Did Aunt Miriam ever—?"

"No. She never came home. She never called. Neither did Vic."

The fact that the sheriff hadn't called was probably a good thing. If he'd found her, it was apt to be...

Rachel let the thought dangle, unwilling to finish the sentence, intent on switching her train of thought. That Aunt Miriam hadn't shown up meant she was either being held somewhere or was hiding. But where? And if she was hiding, why hadn't she gotten a message to Rachel to let her know she was all right?

Lark's hand touched her shoulder, breaking her reverie. "In case Miriam forgot to tell you, Rae, the first Saturday of the month is EPOCH field trip day. Location changes, but anyone who wants to go meets here promptly at eight. Which gives you less than an hour to shower and dress."

Twenty minutes later, Rachel pulled on a pair of jeans and a cotton T-shirt, then braided her hair, Lark fashion, down her back. By the time she'd laced her hiking boots, grabbed a jacket, and reached the kitchen, the sofa bed was folded up and Dorothy, Cecilia, and Gertie were ensconced in the kitchen, gossiping.

"We heard Miriam stayed out last night," said Gertie with a questioning look. Rachel shot Lark a glare.

"Sorry," she mouthed.

Before Rachel could respond, Harry, Forest, and the Hendersons arrived, followed by Eric and Charles, who slipped in through the patio. Lark immediately called the meeting to order. "First order of business. As some of you already know, Miriam never came home yesterday."

A murmuring rose among the birdwatchers, like a small chorus of hummingbirds.

"That's not all," Lark said. "The white gyrfalcon and the two peregrine eyasses are also missing."

The birdwatchers were stunned. Charles looked like fresh vulture stew. Dark circles rimmed his pale eyes. His face was drawn and gray. "Did Miriam call?"

"No," Rachel said, watching him worry his earring. She wondered what type of accident had caused him to lose the tip of his finger. He caught her watching him, and glanced away.

The murmuring crescendoed into shouted questions.

"Doesn't anyone know where she is?"

"Have you called the sheriff yet?"

"What does he think happened to the birds?"

Lark raised her hands for quiet. "Vic thinks Miriam might have the birds, that she might have taken them somewhere. Rachel, Eric and I think it's more likely that she and the birds were kidnapped."

"Now how in the world did you jump to that conclusion?" asked Gertie, a smug look on her face.

"Logic," Rachel snapped. "We couldn't think of any reason for her to take the birds, so—"

"You concocted a reason for someone to steal them?" Gertie fluffed her bobbed hair. "Seems a bit of a stretch to me."

Dorothy waved her hand in the air. "What I want to know is, what in heaven's name is being done?"

"We reported the missing birds to the sheriff," Lark said. "We can't file a missing person's report until tomorrow. Vic's put out an APB on Miriam in connection with the birds, and he's checking the car rental agencies and the airport to see if she changed her travel plans."

"Does he think there's a connection to Donald Bursau's murder?"

"Gertie!" Cecilia's voice shattered the shocked silence blanketing the group. "What are you saying?"

"I'm just asking a question. There are things we don't know, Cecilia. Like, exactly what did Bursau ask Miriam? And what did she say that made him angry enough to storm out of the barn on Monday afternoon?"

Rachel heard the whisper of voices. Ten pairs of eyes focused on her. "Fair enough," she said, standing up. "He was asking a lot of questions."

She recounted the conversation between Miriam and Bursau as she'd heard it, then told the EPOCH members what Miriam had added about Bursau's suspicions of Uncle William.

"That's preposterous," Gertie protested. "My father never—"

"I did some research and talked with Kirk Udall, the new

reporter assigned to the story," Rachel interrupted. "According to him, Bursau had some proof of Uncle William's involvement."

Gertie's face turned a deep shade of red, giving her the appearance of a chocolate-dipped strawberry.

"That's garbage," Charles said. "William Tanager was the most ethical man I ever met."

"I'll second that," Dorothy said, raising her hand again. "He was a great man, one of the greatest ornithologists of all time."

The others nodded.

"That's right," Gertie blurted. "How dare you accuse my father of dishonest behavior?"

Rachel placed her hand against her chest, and shook her head. "I'm not the one doubting Uncle William's integrity. Though, I admit, I'd like to know what Donald Bursau thought he had on him. I hoped it might offer some clue to the killer or birdnapper." And Miriam's kidnapper. The more Rachel thought about it, the more convinced she was that Miriam had surprised the birdnapper at the Raptor House. And that the killer and the birdnapper were one and the same.

"The first thing we need to do is find Miriam," Charles said. "We need to check all the places she might have gone."

"I agree," Harry chimed in.

"Does this mean we're not going birdwatching today?" Cecilia asked.

"Cecilia!" Dorothy exclaimed, jabbing her sister in the ribs.

"I'm just asking." Cecilia batted her sister's elbow away. "You know, I still need the LeConte's sparrow for my life list. And did you hear? Andrew spotted a chestnut-sided warbler down by Elk Lake yesterday."

Andrew nodded. "A singing male. Please please pleased to meet'cha. He was a beaut."

A murmur rose from the gathering.

"Quiet," shouted Lark. She waited for the din to die down. "If you don't want to help, that's fine. It's your choice. Go birdwatching. Otherwise, we need to come up with a plan."

Everyone stayed.

Eventually it was decided that half of them would check the

abandoned cabins dotting the woods edging Rocky Mountain National Park, and the other half would canvass the town, calling on anyone Miriam might turn to for help.

"This is ridiculous," insisted Gertie once the matter was settled. "If Miriam was in trouble, she'd turn to one of us. Who's to say someone isn't already harboring her, or that she hasn't already fled the state?"

Rachel hated to admit it, but both thoughts had occurred to her. Especially in light of Sheriff Garcia's revelation, which made it likely one of the birdwatchers had made the call luring Donald Bursau to his death.

Not that Rachel believed Aunt Miriam capable of killing anyone. But if she knew who had murdered the reporter, she might have felt a need to go underground. But then why hadn't she confided in Rachel? Because she didn't want to place her in danger? Or had she turned to the wrong person? "Doing something—anything—is better than nothing, Gertie."

Several hours later, the EPOCH members reconvened at Bird Haven. No one had had any luck finding Miriam. However, several had spotted the chestnut-sided warbler, and Andrew Henderson had scored a rufous-sided towhee.

"Anyone have any other bright ideas?" Harry asked, slumping onto the stone hearth of the patio barbecue.

"Brainstorming," Forest said. "Now there's a good one." He was settled into a chair next to the table, under the shade of the oversized umbrella.

Gertie curled her lip. "Oh, please! We've discussed all our ideas to death. I say we all go home, and wait and see what Vic comes up with."

"Well, I say we brainstorm," urged Dorothy.

"Me, too," Cecilia agreed, her gaze flitting across the meadow. "Oh, look, there's a male western bluebird."

"Where?" Ten heads swiveled to where Cecilia pointed.

"There. One o'clock, on the fence post."

Rachel straightened up, cupped a hand over her eyes, and squinted. So far the only birds she had spotted while birdwatching were the two in The Thicket, the night they found

Bursau murdered. "I don't see anything."

"There it goes." Harry pointed, arcing his arm through the air.

"It's on the Raptor House barn now," declared Eric. "The eave on the left side."

A flicker of movement caught Rachel's eye. A small blue bird with a rust-colored breast ruffled the shadow. "How can you tell what it is?"

Gertie laughed. "That's rich! She's taking over for Miriam and she can't even ID a western bluebird."

Hot color stung Rachel's cheeks.

"Leave her alone, Gertie," Lark said, turning her back on Rachel's cousin and rolling her eyes. "It's really simple, Rae. Look at the markings and the size first, then try looking through these." She handed Rachel a pair of binoculars. "The male western bluebird is small, deep blue with a rusty-colored breast and a chestnut marking on its back."

It took Rachel a minute or two to find a reference on the Raptor House roof, then lower the binoculars to frame the small bird. She sucked in her breath when the bluebird came into focus close-up. "He's pretty."

"Behavior can tell you a lot, too. See how the bird sort of hunches over?"

Charles cleared his throat. "Do you think you can finish the lesson later? I'd like to get back to business."

Rachel lowered the binoculars. A twinge of guilt gnawed at her conscience. It had felt good to be distracted. "Charles is right. Me three on the brainstorming."

"Good," declared Forest, clapping his hands. "Now, there are any number of methods we can try. There's the arrow method, the bubble method, and the doodle method. Basically, all of them require throwing out ideas, then grouping them into some order based on the problem one is attempting to solve."

The group buzzed.

"I've used clustering," Rachel said. Her boss, Jack Jaffery, swore by the method for coming up with new marketing strategies. "But we need a chalkboard or some large sheets of paper and markers."

Lark pushed herself out of her chair. "I think I know where I can find some."

"You people aren't serious?" asked Gertie, crossing her arms across her chest and plumping her bosom.

"Dead serious," replied Forest. "We're bound to come up with some new ideas on where Miriam is, or on who might have taken the birds and why. It's sort of a mini think tank,"

"I say it's worth a try." Charles's blue eyes dared any of them to disagree. Rachel felt a rush of gratitude at his insistence. Regardless of her feelings about his relationship with Miriam, it was obvious he cared a great deal about her aunt.

The largest sheet of paper Lark could dig up was the back of a calendar page. She taped it to the patio door, dug a large red pen out of a drawer by the kitchen phone, and handed Forest the marker. He handed it to Rachel.

"Do you mind doing the recording? I think better on my feet." He paced, pivoted, and said, "Okay, someone toss out an idea."

"I'll start," Rachel offered. She wrote Miriam, white gyrfalcon, peregrines, and missing in the center of the paper.

"Great. What else comes to mind?" Forest asked. "Anything. How about thoughts on motives?"

"Money," Charles said.

"Ransom," Cecilia said.

Rachel scribbled the words at the top of the page. Miriam had confided that all of her money was tied up in Bird Haven. She was land rich and cash poor. Maybe on paper she was worth more than the birds, but no one, including herself, could access the money.

"Escape," Gertie said, as though reading her mind.

"Really, Gertie!" Dorothy whispered something to Cecilia. Rachel wrote down the word.

"How about danger?" Rachel asked. Even if Aunt Miriam hadn't been kidnapped, she might have seen something, or discovered something that had driven her into hiding. But if that was the case, why hadn't she tried to get word to her? And how had she gotten wherever she was? Her car was still parked out front.

Eric scraped back his chair and walked to the edge of the patio. "It sounds like you think Miriam's guilty of something,

Gertie."

"Maybe I do."

Rachel fought back another onslaught of tears. "Do you think we could stay focused?"

"Gyrfalcon and peregrines make me think of falconry," Andrew said. Opal nodded.

"Propagation," Eric said.

"Mike Johnson," Lark said.

Rachel wrote his name on the paper. She had learned last night that Johnson was the owner of Black Canyon Creek Ranch, the spread just east of Bird Haven. He owned four thousand acres of land and catered to the serious outdoor adventure types. A master falconer, he wielded a lot of power in Elk Park.

"He's an opportunist," Charles said. "I don't know why Miriam agrees to deal with him."

"Because he knows more about raptors than I might forget," Eric said. "He's helped us out a few times, and Miriam feels she owes him."

"He's a money-grubbing capitalist."

"Am I missing something?" Rachel asked. Charles shifted in his chair, crossing his arms and clamping his mouth shut like a petulant child.

"Mike's negotiating with the Bureau of Land Management for a special land-use permit for the Twin Owls area," explained Eric. "He wants to operate a year-round climbing camp."

"Can't he just use the rock like anyone else?"

"Ja, except he wants to expand his operation. He wants to run the rock like a ski area, offering instruction, employing climbing patrols, that sort of thing. He plans to designate beginner, intermediate, and expert areas, and make sort of an outdoor climbing gym."

"What does any of that have to do with Aunt Miriam?"

"Nothing, except that years ago, she granted him a temporary easement to tie his driveway into Raptor House Road. It's the current access to Twin Owls, and some people think"—he shot a pointed glance in Charles's direction—"if she rescinds Mike's easement and converts Raptor House Road back to a private drive, it would prevent Mike from obtaining the BLM land-use permit."

Was that why Lark had been so adamant that Miriam needed to stop allowing the public access to Rocky Mountain National Park through Bird Haven? And how would rescinding the easement affect the land status in relation to the stipulations in Uncle William's will?

"Lumpy Ridge is open for climbing use now, isn't it?"

"That's just it." Eric pulled a small map of Rocky Mountain National Park from his back pocket and pointed to Lumpy Ridge. "Right now the park closes this area to climbing during the raptor nesting season. We think there's at least one active peregrine nest on Twin Owls."

"If Mike gets permission to open his camp," Lark explained, "the nesting pair will be driven out."

"As if the BLM bureaucrats care," Charles said with a snort. "If Johnson waves enough money under their noses, they'll give him whatever he wants."

"I agree." Harry spoke for the first time since they'd started brainstorming. "The only thing that'll stop Mike is someone hitting him hard in the pocketbook, like Miriam shutting down access so he's forced to find an alternate route."

Forest paced the floor. "I have a different approach. I'm sponsoring a bill in Congress this year that would restrict access to federal lands providing habitat for endangered wildlife."

"As EPOCH members, we all agree some regulation is critical to maintaining wildlife habitat," stated Gertie. It was the first time Rachel agreed with her. "It's the level of regulation needed that's open for debate. Naturally, Mike Johnson vehemently opposes the whole premise."

"Everyone agrees that maintaining our wilderness boundaries is crucial to preserving an environment for our wildlife, Forest." Charles leaned forward. "The Nettleman Bill is great in that it restricts commercial use, allows area closures based on wildlife activity, and bans expeditions into the wilderness in certain habitat areas. Where it falls apart is the policy on backcountry permits."

Forest stopped pacing. "Not everyone agrees with you on that." He turned to Rachel. "You see, under my bill only a limited number of guided excursions will be allowed, and only a limited number of guide permits will be issued triannually. Environmental impact is curtailed by requiring all backcountry visitors to use guide services, and all guides to donate a percentage of their annual profits to the Park Service for upkeep of the National Park System."

"But it means none of us can go birdwatching in the backcountry without guide services," complained Andrew. Opal nodded.

"That may be," Forest agreed. "But on a national level, the Nettleman Bill has been well received among environmentalists and animal rights activists alike—educated people who realize that damage done to our wildlife habitat is damage to our heritage. Educated people willing to sacrifice individual gratification for the sake of humanity. The time has come when society as a whole must throw a monkey wrench into the gears and stop the pillage and rape of our natural resources. How? By stopping advancement into our wilderness areas."

"Thank you, Forest." Gertie clapped her hands loudly. "Now hush up and sit down."

To Rachel, Forest sounded like a People for the Ethical Treatment of the Earth advocate. Not that she was against PETE per se, just that radicals on either side of the fence frightened the hell out of her. A similar faction called the Earth Liberation Front recently claimed responsibility for fires at Vail causing twelve million dollars' worth of damage before the opening of the season. ELF threatened more attacks as long as Vail put forth continued plans for ski area expansion into possible lynx habitat.

Forest sat down with a parting shot. "Mike Johnson wants to see the Nettleman Bill shot down."

"Of course he does," Lark said, "though you'd think the lummox would realize that he stands to make a truckload of money when he snags one of the guide permits. Either way, he comes out a winner and the rest of us lose."

It was easy to see that Lark didn't care much for Mike Johnson, and that she didn't agree with the provisions of the Nettleman Bill. Rachel wondered how the rest of them felt.

Andrew had pegged it right. If the bill passed, it would certainly limit EPOCH's birdwatching treks into the backcountry. They might even be forced to hire Mike Johnson as a birding guide. Push them hard enough, and EPOCH might come to stand for Environmentalists Plotting Overt Crimes for Habitat.

Rachel opted to backtrack. "Someone Johnson said was a falconer. Does he have a propagation permit?"

Lark narrowed her eyes. "I don't think so. Why?"

"From what Eric told me, the peregrines' greatest value is to someone needing new breeding stock, right?"

"Ja, but falconries are heavily regulated in Colorado," Eric said, seeming to follow her train of thought. "They're subject to spot checks at any time. Johnson would be taking too big a risk if he kept stolen birds in his mews."

"Mews?" Birders should come with glossaries.

"Cages," Gertie explained.

"Then Johnson has the facilities to keep birds."

"Not really." Eric leaned back and crossed his legs. "A master falconer is limited to three birds; therefore he needs only three cages. If his birds are lost or they die, he can't take more than three birds from the wild in replacement. And he'd have to obtain special permits to take those."

"Peregrines aren't legal," Harry said.

"Mike could purchase birds," Eric continued, "but then they're registered and banded. He's not stupid enough to steal birds and try to house them, too."

"No, but he's arrogant enough to try it temporarily," Lark said.

She sounded like she had firsthand knowledge of Mike Johnson. Rachel made a mental note to ask her more about him when they were alone.

"Who conducts spot checks, Eric?" Harry asked.

"Ian Ogburn, U.S. Fish and Wildlife."

Harry pulled a pair of glasses from his pocket and knuckled them into place on his nose. "Do you have his number?"

"Ja, out in the truck."

Eric left to get the number, and Rachel glanced around at the birdwatchers. Their body language was clear. Forest slouched in a chair, arms crossed over his chest. Harry scratched notes on a small spiral pad. Andrew and Opal whispered with Cecilia and Dorothy. Lark sulked, and Gertie studied them all with the same open curiosity Rachel was exhibiting. Charles stared into space, his legs crossed, an unreadable expression etched on his face. Rachel decided he was either plotting sabotage or worrying about Aunt Miriam.

"I have just one more question," Rachel said. "Based on what Eric said, why would a man of Johnson's standing take the risks involved in stealing the falcons?"

Lark answered. "The man caters to eccentricity. His clients are all rich guys who know what they want, the cost be damned. Mike Johnson's what I'd call a risk junkie."

That sounded a lot like someone else Rachel knew. Her gaze wandered toward the Raptor House, and an image of Roger wavered at the edge of the meadow. She closed her eyes tight. She had more important things to think about.

Like the fact that Aunt Miriam was missing.

Chapter 9

When Rachel opened her eyes, the apparition materialized. Only it wasn't Roger. Instead, a Clark Kent look-alike with a skimpy goatee strode toward her, holding up a copy of the Elk Park Gazette.

"Way to go, Rachel Stanhope," he said as he reached the patio. "You're front page news."

"Who are you?" Rachel demanded.

"Kirk Udall, Birds of a Feather magazine, at your service." He flashed white teeth. "I thought you'd be happier to see me. Actually, I was hoping you'd decided to trade me back rubs."

Rachel snatched the paper from his hand, torn between smacking him with it as if he were a naughty puppy and reading the headline. "Let me see that."

She scanned the headline. Body Found in the Thicket was inked in 42-point type. And an ingenious staff reporter must have downloaded Rachel's head shot from the Images Plus website, because her picture was pasted in the center of the layout. The caption read, Summer resident, Rachel Stanhope, stumbles over murder.

"Read it," Gertie said.

Rachel skimmed the copy silently. The first half recounted the events of Thursday evening. The second half moved into the realm of speculation.

Local resident Miriam Tanager's the prime suspect in the murder, and she is reported to be the last person to see donald bursau alive. it is believed that bursau, an investigative reporter for Birds of a Feather magazine, was in town researching a story on Tanager's late husband, William, the renowned ornithologist who had called Elk Park home since the late 1970s.

Several paragraphs detailed Uncle Will's childhood, his graduation from Northwestern University, his subsequent move to Elk Park, and his career highlights.

Just hours after a visit to Bird Haven, Donald Bursau returned to Elk Park, and checked out of his room at the Drummond Hotel.

Rachel glanced at Lark. Why hadn't she said anything about Bursau's staying at the Drummond? Rachel had assumed he was staying at one of the cheaper hotels. Her gaze drifted back to the newspaper.

A subsequent search of the premises turned up no clues, but sources close to the police investigation confirm that Bursau's car was discovered abandoned in Rocky mountain national Park late this afternoon. The trunk contained luggage, computer equipment, and an empty computer disk box. Further investigation showed that several files stored on the computer had been overwritten around the time of death.

"Are you going to read it out loud, or not?" Gertie asked. She stepped forward and extended a hand to Udall. "You must be the reporter they've sent to replace Mr. Bursau. I'm Gertie Tanager, the daughter of the man you're doing the exposé on."

Rachel shoved the paper between Gertie's fingers, making it awkward for the reporter to shake her hand. "They say something about 'the members of a local bird club,' and talk about Miriam, Will, and Charles. Why don't you read it for yourself?"

Udall grinned. "Guess you didn't expect to see me so soon. After your phone call, I decided there must be more of a story here than I'd realized."

"You're saying murder isn't enough?" Rachel sized him up. Dressed like an L.L. Bean model, Udall looked like a nature nut to her. Maybe he cared only about nonhuman species.

"The murder raised a few eyebrows, but there are a lot of people connected to a lot of other stories who might have wanted Bursau dead."

Charles turned to Gertie. "What do they say about me in that article?"

"You're noted as being Daddy's oldest friend," Gertie said. "But I can't believe they didn't mention the rest of us. We were all there, every last one of us, except for you two." She gestured toward the Hendersons, who were donning their jackets.

"We need to be going," Opal said. Rachel thanked the couple for their efforts to locate Miriam, and escorted them out through the house. By the time she returned to the patio, Eric had come back with Ian Ogburn's number and he, Udall, and the others were busy dissecting the article. And they were all calling Udall "Kirk."

Eric gestured at the newspaper. "This doesn't look good."

Rachel agreed, but she wasn't sure if she wanted to discuss it in front of Kirk Udall. If Bursau was the Geraldo of the bird world, who was to say Udall wasn't the Jerry Springer?

Granted, the missing computer disks, assuming there were ten there, and the overwritten files pointed to motive. Someone wanted something kept under wraps. But who? Aunt Miriam? Given the fact that Bursau's investigation had focused on Bird Haven and Uncle Will's alleged illegal activities, there was no doubt that Sheriff Garcia would leap to that conclusion.

"Will someone explain what this means, 'several files stored on the computer had been overwritten'?" Dorothy underlined the words with a pink-tipped finger.

Rachel sat down on one of the stools. "It's one way of erasing files from a computer hard drive. Given the right tools, a deleted file can be retrieved. But on an overwritten file the existing information is written over, making it virtually impossible to recover."

"Why would the killer go to all that trouble?" Lark asked. "Why not just steal the computer, or trash it?"

Good question. Rachel considered possible reasons and came up with one. "Because the killer didn't overwrite the files."

"Then who did?" Dorothy asked.

"Bursau might have done it himself for some reason. Maybe he thought someone was trying to steal them." Rachel fingered a strand of her hair. "What kind of a guy was he... Kirk?"

"Anal, totally. I'd bet he backed up his files—"

"On the missing computer disks!" blurted Charles, perking up a little.

It made sense to Rachel. "Bursau was frightened. He warned Aunt Miriam to be careful. I'll bet he thought he was in danger, too."

"He was right," Udall said.

"So what are you guys saying?" Lark asked. "That Bursau stored the information on disks and cleaned his hard drive?"

"It's a possibility," Rachel said.

"I'd say it's safe to assume the killer now has those disks," Kirk said.

"Oh please," Rachel drawled, adopting one of Gertie's lines. "For all we know the killer's still looking for them." That might have been what she'd heard in the bushes the night she'd found Bursau's body—the killer searching the area for the missing disks days after the murder.

Harry looked at her over the top of his glasses. "What type of files would use a whole set of disks to store information?"

"Photographs." Rachel had figured that out almost immediately. She worked with graphic files day in and day out, storing most of her own on zip drive disks. Saving pictures on a hard drive slowed down the machine, making it harder to use certain programs. "Digital pictures eat a lot of bytes."

"We know Bursau received a call from Bird Haven on Monday, before he checked out of the hotel," Lark said. "The question is from whom?"

"It seems safe to assume—"

Rachel shot Kirk a scathing glance. "That it was one of us, or Mike Johnson arranging to meet him—"

"In order get their hands on the disks," Lark finished.

"Oh, my," Dorothy said. "Who would do that?"

The killer. Rachel combed her fingers through her hair, pushing it away from her face. "Sheriff Garcia would say Aunt Miriam."

"That's pure speculation," Forest said. "For all we know, the person called to offer him more information." He looked pointedly at Gertie.

Charles cleared his throat. "Miriam told me she was going to call Bursau." His voice was barely audible. "She wanted to buy his silence in regard to Will."

Rachel stepped toward him. Eric placed a restraining hand on her arm.

"Why didn't you tell us this earlier, Charles?" she asked.

He shot Rachel a defiant glare. "I gave Miriam my word I'd keep quiet. I tried to talk her out of it. I told her not to call. I was, I still am, convinced that reporter was trying to blackmail her."

Rachel glanced at Kirk Udall. The man had one heck of a poker face.

Quiet blanketed the patio. Lark sloshed coffee into a mug. Finally she broke the silence. "Okay, let's say Bursau agreed to meet Miriam, give her the disks, and erase his computer files. She had time to pick them up on her way to The Thicket Monday night. Remember, she drove down alone. Rae stayed home that night."

Cecilia pulled a tissue from her purse and blotted her upper lip. "This is getting serious."

Getting? One man is dead and Aunt Miriam is missing, and she thinks it's getting serious?

"Where do you suppose the disks are now?" asked Udall.

Leave it to him to ask the obvious question.

"Maybe Miriam stashed them somewhere in the house."

Or maybe she took them with her when she left.

Eric slid his chair back. It screeched on the patio stones. "If someone knew Miriam had the disks, they might have tried searching the cages to find them."

"Or maybe they wanted to hide them somewhere," Harry said, dusting his hands together.

"Or maybe someone just killed two birds with one stone," Rachel said.

The birders glared.

"Sorry, no pun intended." Rachel looked down at her hands and played with her fingers. Here's the church, here's the steeple. Open the doors and see all the people. Only in this case it was a barn. "Bursau was doing a story on bird trafficking, right? So doesn't it stand to reason that the bird traffickers wanted both the disks and the birds?"

Dorothy fidgeted with her tissue. "Why on earth would Miriam get herself involved in something so dangerous?"

"To protect Will," Cecilia declared. "I would do almost anything to protect my Jim." That was saying a lot, considering her husband had been missing in action for over forty-seven years.

Harry coughed.

Lark stirred her coffee, licked the spoon, then pointed it toward the other birders. "That's probably why Kirk's friend Bursau exited stage left, and checked out with no advance notice." She cast a guilty look at Rachel.

Rachel decided to let her wallow in it.

"Then who shot him?" Eric asked.

"Who cares?" Lark responded. "The point is, if Miriam had what she wanted, she had no reason to kill the guy."

"Unless he planned to report what he knew anyway," Kirk said. "Maybe she figured Bursau was lying."

Rachel glared at him. "We're operating under the assumption that Aunt Miriam is innocent, Kirk."

"Duly noted." He gave a rakish smile that tugged at her resolve to remain annoyed with him.

"How many disks does a box of computer disks hold?" Harry asked. "Assuming it was full."

"Usually ten," Rachel answered.

Lark's head came up. Her spoon clanged on the counter. "If Miriam has even one of the disks…"

Rachel locked eyes with her. "Then she's got a clue to Bursau's killer."

Lark nodded. "Which means—"

"Your aunt Miriam's got herself in deep doo-doo," Udall said.

After a cursory search of the Raptor House and Bird Haven turned up nothing, the discussion petered out around three o'clock. Miriam had been missing nearly twenty-four hours. Rachel watched the others prepare to leave with growing apprehension. She didn't want to wait for word from Aunt Miriam all alone.

The consensus of the EPOCH members was that whoever'd

killed Bursau had most likely come after Miriam. The hope was that she had something the killer wanted, and there would be some type of ransom request, or else that she had fled and was hiding out. But if that was the case, why hadn't she called?

Fear for Miriam's safety and a need for company drove Rachel into town for dinner. Two chocolate milkshakes and bellyache later, she drove back to Bird Haven, checked the voicemail, and went to bed.

Hours later, she woke with a start. Her heart pounded, sweat beaded her brow. She reached to touch the pillow beside her, then remembered where she was.

Something was wrong! She pushed back the comforter and sat up. What had wakened her? She didn't remember having a bad dream.

The wind gusted outside, stirring the trees. A branch tapped against the windowpane. She exhaled. Just another new sound to contend with.

In New York she'd learned to tune out the noise—the blare of horns, the squeal of tires, the clatter of construction, and the endless prattle of voices on the street outside her window. And, until two months ago, Roger snoring softly beside her in bed.

In Elk Park, she was learning to sleep alone and to contend with the sounds of silence—quiet so intense she heard pine needles brushing glass, wood snapping with temperature changes, and the voices of her soul. She'd been here only six nights, but already she'd learned to differentiate ranch house noises.

A floorboard creaked.

Rachel's breath caught in her throat. Her pulse quickened. That was the sound of someone walking—upstairs. There was someone inside the house!

Maybe Aunt Miriam had come home. Rachel swung her legs over the side of the bed. Miriam was a light sleeper, and she paced the floors at night. Rachel heard her whenever she stepped into the hall and creaked down the stairs for hot chocolate.

But she would have seen Rachel's note. If it was Miriam, why hadn't she wakened Rachel when she came in?

She jammed her feet into a pair of fleece-lined slippers, and pulled a robe over her flannel nightshirt. It was just a little before two o'clock. Whoever was prowling around upstairs didn't belong there.

Rachel eased open the bedroom door, forming a silent prayer that it wouldn't squeak and that whoever was in the house was someone she wouldn't mind meeting in a dark alley. She inched her way slowly down the hall, feeling her way by trailing her fingers along the rough-board wall. Pine scent assailed her nostrils. Her heart throbbed in her ears.

She stopped at the end of the hall. She could see the stairway, and the landing halfway to the first floor. Moonlight streaked the walls in barlike patterns of white and black. Then the shadow of someone descending the stairs fell across the hardwood floor.

She pressed against the splintery boards and squinted in the darkness, trying to identify the person padding down the carpeted steps. Too tall to be Aunt Miriam, and most likely a man, judging by the way he held his arms.

A white blur flew at her face, and she flung her arms up, emitting a sharp squeak. Perky! Damn!

The person on the stairs froze, then bolted, taking the stairs two at a time.

Instinct told Rachel to run for the study, lock the door, and dial 911. Self-defense training told her to be aggressive. The intruder knew she had seen him. Turning tail would only give away the fact she was terrified, and give him the advantage.

As Grandma Wilder always said, the best offense is to kick him where it hurts. If the prowler came within range, Rachel planned to karate chop his balls off.

She fumbled for the light switch. "Stop!"

The lights flared on. A flash of blue bolted into the living room.

Shit! What now? What if he's not alone?

Rachel succumbed to instinct, grabbed the hall telephone, and punched in 911.

"What's your emergency?"

"There's someone in my house."

"I'm having trouble hearing you, Miss."

"That's because I'm whispering." She didn't want the intruder to double back and stop her from placing the call. "There is someone in my house."

"I'm sorry, Miss, but you'll have to speak up."

"Send help. There's an intruder who doesn't belong here."

"Did you say there is someone in your house?"

"Yes." Did the dispatcher have delayed response syndrome?

"You have an intruder?"

"Yes, yes."

"Hold the line, Miss. I'll dispatch someone to the scene, but it may take a few minutes. Can you confirm your address for me?"

"Bird Haven. I'm at Bird Haven." Rachel set the receiver down on the table. While the dispatcher dinked around, the intruder was getting away, and he was a possible link to Aunt Miriam's whereabouts.

"Are you still there, Miss?" The dispatcher's voice rasped through the receiver. "Please remain on the line!"

Rachel didn't answer. A door slammed at the rear of the house.

Think, Stanhope! She hadn't heard a car engine, so the intruder was still on foot, and therefore still on the grounds. Was he still in the house? Had he slammed the door to trick her into believing he'd slipped out the back?

The thought chilled her. Anyone willing to enter an occupied house to steal something was a person on the edge. Had whoever'd come here tonight known she was home?

Rachel moved cautiously into the living room. She crossed the room, fearful of the lurking shadows. Grabbing a poker from the set of fireplace tools, she balanced it on her shoulder like a baseball bat and started up the short flight of steps leading to the dining room.

A sharp whistle caused her to jump. Perky flew in, lit on the mantel, and whistled again.

"Shut up!" whispered Rachel, hyperventilating into her cupped hands.

Make me, said the bird.

Don't tempt me, you little tweet. She brandished the poker in his direction. Where the hell was the sheriff?

She climbed another step. The stair creaked. Rachel froze. If the intruder was still inside and hadn't heard her arguing with the stupid parakeet, he couldn't have missed the squeaky step. Alerting him to her whereabouts didn't seem like a great idea. On the other hand, if he'd slammed out the back door, he was getting away.

Be bold, Stanhope. Quit mincing your way along. Rachel raised the poker and charged into the dining room. She glanced left, then right. Not a soul was there.

Perky flew up the parallel staircase on the opposite side of the fireplace and perched on a candlestick. Problem, Chicky Baby?

"I don't suppose you'd tell me if you saw someone circling around."

Nope.

Rachel flipped off the bird, then moved stealthily toward the cozy area attached to the dining room. She passed the swinging door that led to the kitchen. It didn't slam, and the kitchen doors to the patio slid open and thumped closed. The cozy area off the dining room had the only door in this part of the house that slammed. It exited onto the back patio.

The door was shut tight, but unlocked. Rachel drew a deep breath, exhaled, and flipped on the patio lights. A figure loomed in the window.

Chapter 10

Eric stepped forward and pressed his nose to the glass. Rachel yanked open the door. Forest and Charles rushed forward, flanking him from behind.

"What in God's name are you doing here?" she demanded, wielding the fireplace poker in anger.

Eric's gaze traveled along the piece of metal and rested on the hooked end. He took a step back. "We were installing some security measures, and heard your call on the scanner. Are you okay?"

"Did you see anyone running away from here when you came up from the barn?" Rachel peered past him into the night that encircled the patio with a curtain of black. The three men looked at each other and shook their heads.

"Nope," Eric said. "We didn't see a soul."

Sheriff Garcia surveyed the chaos in the study and shook his head. "You sure you didn't hear anything?"

Rachel stared in horror at the emptied drawers, slashed cushions, and strewn desk contents littering the floor. She swallowed to steady her voice. "Positive. But you can't hear anything from my room. I heard something only when the person stepped into the hall. Because of the board that creaks."

"Was the person carrying anything?"

"Not that I could see. His hands were free."

Sheriff Garcia rubbed the ends of his mustache. "He could've stuffed something small in his pocket. You say he was headed down?"

"When I reached the hallway, he was on the stairs."

"And that's when you flipped on the lights."

"Right."

"And what did he do then?"

"He ran." Rachel squelched her annoyance at his line of questioning. It was a common marketing strategy to repeat information. The rule of thumb was to repeat things a minimum of three times for maximum retention. In the last four days, she'd decided that it must be a Sheriff's Department strategy to rephrase and requestion witnesses as many times as needed to get the answers the sheriff wanted to hear. Garcia was into round five. He should have gotten the answers by now.

Garcia turned to the three men. "And none of you saw anything?"

Forest responded first. "No, like we told you, Sheriff, we were wiring a security system. Eric heard the call over the scanner, shouted to Charles and me, and we all ran up to the house."

"You were together the whole time?"

"Yes," Charles said. "Out in the Raptor House wiring a security system to protect the buildings from break-in."

"Together?"

"Yes." The three men nodded in unison.

"And you were wiring this system at two o'clock in the morning."

"That's right, Sheriff," Eric said. "We've already lost three birds. I don't relish losing any more."

"I'll be the first to admit it's taken us longer than we had anticipated," Forest said, pressing a fist to his hip. "Are you going somewhere with this line of questioning, Vic? It's apparent something's on your mind. Perhaps you'd like to enlighten the rest of us."

Garcia gestured to the uniformed officers working the crime scene that he was stepping outside, then signaled for Eric, Forest, Charles, and Rachel to join him in the hall. The floorboard squeaked as he stepped through the doorway. He stopped, then bounced up and down, making it creak several times more. "From what you've told me, the three of you were in separate parts of the Raptor House. Could you actually see each other?"

"Not always," Eric admitted.

"But you were in constant communication?"

"Not constant," Charles said. "Get to the point, Sheriff. What are you driving at?"

"I'm just trying to establish your alibis. We already know that one of you"—he raised his palms—"one of the birdwatchers made a call to Bursau from here on the night of the murder."

Forest puffed out his cheeks in indignation. "Are you suggesting Eric, Charles, or I might have come up here and rifled Miriam's study?"

"No, I'm just verifying your whereabouts."

"This is ludicrous," Charles said. "Even if one of us wanted to come in here, none of us would be stupid enough to risk being seen. Rachel would have recognized any one of us."

Garcia swung his head back and forth. "Not in the dark."

"I heard her say she turned on the lights," Forest pointed out.

"Yes, but the intruder was running by then. She saw a flash of blue, then he disappeared through the darkened living room."

The sheriff's suggestion was chilling. Could it have been one of these men? Rachel's gaze traveled over the threesome. All of them wore blue jeans.

"This is utter rubbish. Hell, I could no more outrun this young girl than I could outrun Deputy Fife over there." Charles gestured at a young deputy squatting near the door.

"You play tennis twice a week, Pendergast. And you work out at the club. I think you underestimate yourself." The sheriff grinned. "What do you think, Ma'am?"

Rachel didn't know what to think. Or, for that matter, whom to trust anymore. "I fail to see a motive."

Garcia rubbed his chin. "Why?"

"Because he was obviously after the computer disks," Charles said, plopping down on the hallway settee, "and we'd already searched for them up here this afternoon."

"What do you know about the computer disks?" Garcia asked suspiciously. He eyed each of them, petting his mustache

Finally, Rachel spoke up. "I know only what was mentioned in the newspaper. Or rather not mentioned." She related how Kirk Udall had shown up with the paper, and how they'd come up with the hypothesis about Bursau's selling out his story. "Of course, it's only a theory."

"You say this new reporter's here, in town?" Garcia signaled to the deputy dusting the door for fingerprints. "Go and bring in a fella by the name of Kirk Udall for questioning. Find out if he has an alibi for tonight."

The deputy departed immediately.

"He was here earlier," Rachel said. "I don't see what he would gain by coming back and doing this."

"What would any of you have to gain?" Garcia rubbed his forehead and stared at the carpet. "Did this Udall fellow say anything about receiving any files on disks from Bursau?"

"No."

"Nothing sent by e-mail?"

"He didn't say." Rachel pondered this new line of questioning. Most companies were online, so it made more sense if Bursau e-mailed his notes to the office. In which case, the disks probably served as his version of hard copy. Or as a way to deliver information to the highest bidder.

The sheriff finger-combed his mustache. "Thanks for the tip about Udall. I'll check him out, and call his editor on Monday."

"You never answered Rachel's question, Vic," said Charles.

"What question is that?"

"What possible reason do you think any of us would have for rifling Miriam's study?"

The sheriff slapped his hand against the butt of his gun and pointed at Charles. "The way I see it, Charles, you would do almost anything to protect Miriam."

Even murder someone? Rachel studied the man carefully. His gray hair was cut in military fashion: short, clean around the ears. His blue eyes glinted like steel. "You're right, Vic. I would."

"And Eric might be protecting her, too, though I think he's more apt to be protecting the Raptor House." Garcia balanced on the balls of his feet, then settled back on his heels. "With three birds missing and one guy dead, I figure he's got to be worried about keeping his job. Throw in a whiff of illegal activity, and the feds are apt to close down the operation out here."

Eric's face hardened. His lips paled. It was clear Garcia had struck a nerve.

"And what's my motive, Sheriff?" asked Forest. He appeared to be genuinely curious. And, for that matter, so was Rachel.

"Now that's another matter. I think you're somewhere on the

other side. Whereas these three are looking to avoid a scandal, you want to expose the wrongdoing to the world."

"What good would that do anyone?" asked Rachel

"For starters, it ends access to Rocky Mountain National Park through your aunt's land," Garcia said. "I've been doing some research. It seems that after William Tanager died, your aunt tied the public access to the trailheads at the back of her property to the park's operation of the Raptor House."

That was a new wrinkle, but from what Forest had told them about his pending legislation, denying access through Bird Haven played heavily in his favor. "Sheriff, do you know that Mike Johnson was up here on Monday night and could have placed that telephone call?"

"I am aware of that."

"Then let me ask you a question. You suspect that my aunt, and maybe an accomplice, murdered Bursau, stole the three birds from the Raptor House, and then disappeared, correct?"

"Not exactly. I just haven't eliminated any of the suspects yet."

"So we're all considered suspects?"

The sheriff nodded. "I guess you could say that."

"Then why would my aunt's accomplice tear apart her study? Wouldn't Aunt Miriam have just told him where to look for whatever it is she wanted?"

The sheriff massaged the back of his neck. "I thought of that. You have a point."

"What I think this break-in proves is that Aunt Miriam has something somebody wants. Something somebody would go to great lengths to get."

"Maybe even that Udall fellow," Forest had regained some of his composure. "If Bursau sold out the story, that's reason enough for Udall to want to retrieve the disks."

"Maybe even see Bursau dead," Eric added.

"Or," Garcia said, "that might be how someone wants it to look."

Rachel had heard enough. It seemed like the sheriff twisted everything to make Aunt Miriam look guilty. And Rachel hated to believe one of the EPOCH members was involved. The thought of one of them being a murderer made her stomach flip-flop. With her brother, Ben, in Alaska, her father and grandmother in Chicago, and Miriam missing, the EPOCH members were all she had. "Do you really think Aunt Miriam killed that man?"

"No. I'm just trying to find out where she is."

"That's all I'm asking," Rachel said, exhaling loudly. Somehow they had to be missing something. Something important. But what?

She replayed the scenes leading up to this point: the argument between Miriam and Bursau, pushing through The Thicket, Lark hissing, stumbling over the dead man's foot, two birds flushing, one flying away. What was she forgetting? The bird! It had had something gripped in its beak. And she'd seen a flash of light. "That's it!"

Garcia's eye's narrowed. "What's it?"

"The night I found the body. I saw two birds come up out of the bush. One was the LeConte's sparrow. He settled back down. But the raven carried something off. I'm sure of it."

The three bird experts exchanged glances. The sheriff cocked his head. "My men are just about finished, Rachel. I suggest you try and get some sleep tonight. I'll post a man outside."

"Wait a minute. Aren't any of you interested?"

Garcia laid a hand on her shoulder. "I know you're worried about your aunt, but there's no possible way for me to investigate all the crows—"

"Ravens."

"—that we have around here. If that bird carried something off, it's gone."

Rachel cinched the belt of her robe more tightly around her waist. "I remember seeing a flash of light. I can almost picture it in my mind. There must be some way of tracking that bird."

Garcia spread his arms wide. "How 'bout it? Any of you have any ideas?"

"It would be impossible," agreed Charles. Forest concurred.

"Sorry, Rachel." Garcia paused halfway through the doorway to Miriam's study. "Let me know if you figure out a way. You never know. I've caught a few jailbirds in my day that I thought would get away."

Heat edged its way up Rachel's neck. Granted, it was a slim lead. But she intended to follow it up. "In that case, Sheriff, you might want to talk to Perky. He saw the intruder, too."

The others left right after the sheriff. Rachel waited until the early rays of sunlight tipped the mountain peaks golden, then called Harry. If anyone knew something about ravens, she reasoned, Harry would. He had agreed to stop by.

Now, seated at the breakfast table, he worried his fingers along the handle of his stoneware coffee mug. "You know that your idea's a little out there."

"The others thought so, too. But it is possible, right?"

"Technically, sure. Ravens are members of the corvid family. Plenty strong enough to carry off a computer disk. An adult weighs three or four pounds, and has about a four-foot wingspan."

"Would you define corvid in layman's terms for me?"

"It's a family name, a family being comprised of a number of similar species. The corvid family includes magpies, jays, rooks, and crows."

"All the camp robbers."

"Right. They're the Navajo of the bird world. Adaptable, smart, quick to learn, and great scavengers."

"Tell me about the raven."

"They're the largest species of corvid, and they've been known to pick up odd things."

"What kinds of things?" Rachel hoped computer disks were on the list.

"Candy bars, car keys, shiny objects." Harry leaned back in the chair. "National Geographic did an article on ravens in one of their January issues. Very interesting. The author claimed a raven had unzipped his backpack and stolen his cheese."

"Seriously?"

"Yeah. Then he questioned a biologist in Yellowstone. According to the expert, ravens have been caught opening Velcro fasteners on the snowmobile storage compartments, and even untied knots to snitch food. The article showed a picture of one holding a map."

"So it is possible!" Rachel sloshed her coffee in her excitement, and grabbed for the paper towels. "Assuming the raven did pick up a disk, where would he have carried it?"

Harry helped her blot up the spill. "Most likely he dropped it when he found it wasn't edible."

That left a lot of territory to search between The Thicket and Lumpy Ridge. "Assuming he didn't drop it, where would he have taken it?"

Harry rested his elbows on the table, set his chin in the vee of his hands, and patted his cheeks in thought. "I can think of only two possibilities. Ravens are like golden eagles in that they cache food."

"What do you mean?"

"They bury it, like a dog. They dig a hole in the dirt, drop in a morsel, then cover the spot to hide it. It's rare to locate a cache. The other possibility is finding its nest. It's late in the season, so most of the raven young have hatched by now. Most have fledged. Still, I think it's your best bet." He frowned. "You know, finding one bird in a rant of ravens will be like finding the longest branch on a tree."

A rant of ravens. What had Aunt Miriam called them the day Rachel had misidentified a group as crows? An unkindness of ravens. Maybe this one was kinder than it realized.

"Was there anything unusual about the bird?" Harry asked.

Rachel shut her eyes and tried hard to remember. She tried viewing the memory the way she'd study a photograph. The bird flew. The last rays of sunlight bounced off whatever was in his beak, and on his leg. Her eyes flashed open. "Could he have been banded?"

"We've banded a few." Harry thought a moment. "You said the bird flew to Lumpy Ridge?"

"In that general direction. Toward the camel's back formation."

"Twin Owls formation," he corrected, sitting up. "The park conducts a annual raptor observation program to document the nesting sites up there. Last year some volunteers were asked to record any bird activity, and a lot of the records included other sightings. We could check this year's accountings for a nesting raven."

Rachel felt a resurgence of excitement. Maybe there was still some hope of finding the disk. "Where are the records kept?"

"In the Raptor House."

After a short walk, they were rooting around in Eric's office. Harry came up with the set of binders containing the documentation on nests in the Lumpy Ridge area.

Rachel groaned. "There must be thirty notebooks here."

"Grab a stack."

She followed his lead, skimming the daily reports for any notations of raven sightings. She found several, but none that offered any details. After half an hour, Harry jabbed at a page in his notebook. "Eric located a raven's nest on Twin Owls this year, and he marked the bird as banded."

"Let me see."

Eric had drawn a diagram of the nest location beside his notes. The penciled sketch showed the nest perched on an overhanging ledge near the top of the Lower Owl formation on Twin Owls.

"I think this is your best chance. You can see the Lower Owl from almost anywhere on the property. Set up a scope, keep your eyes open. With luck, maybe you'll spot your bird."

Rachel impulsively hugged him. Harry blushed, and extricated himself. "Don't go overboard. More than likely you won't get what you're after."

"Why do you say that?"

"Even if you're lucky and you spot the bird and find its nest, you can't climb up there."

"Why not?"

"The Owls are off-limits because of the peregrines nesting. Climbers scare the birds. Lumpy Ridge is shut down from now until the end of June, maybe early July."

"I'll bet that makes the climbers happy."

"Most are okay with it. We've had a few threaten to shoot the raptors. More than likely, that's what happened to the eyasses' mother."

The mention of the stolen chicks reminded Rachel of Aunt Miriam's disappearance, and she removed the page with the diagram from the notebook. "The sheriff can climb up there."

"But he won't." Harry raked his hair back. "Trust me. It would be political suicide for him. The sheriff is an elected official, and we're coming up on an election year. Around here the green vote's crucial. Besides, he needs the support of the townspeople for his juvenile delinquent camp. He isn't going to do anything to mess that up."

"I hear what you're saying, Harry, but Aunt Miriam's been missing almost two days. What if she's hurt or needs our help? I can't just sit here and do nothing. If anything happened to her, I'd never forgive myself." Rachel folded the paper and stuck it in her back pocket. "If I spot the bird, the sheriff will have to listen."

"Maybe." Harry stood up, then started for the door. "Let me know how it goes."

Chapter 11

Harry had left, and Eric never showed up for work. Rachel decided to put her own work on hold, borrowed a pair of binoculars from the office, and dragged a lawn chair around the side of the house. There was a good view of Lower Owl from there. Maybe she'd spot the raven.

She settled down in the chair and tried adjusting the binoculars. First, she maneuvered the spacing between the two barrels, then, once she had gauged the distance correctly, focused the image, using the wheel on top of the glasses. The image blurred. She lowered the binoculars, feeling dizzy and sick to her stomach.

Lark pulled into the driveway, and Rachel tried training the binoculars on her.

"Having trouble?" called Lark, climbing out of her car and slamming the door. She walked toward Rachel, a blurry blob of blue, red, and yellow.

Rachel lowered the glasses again. The sun radiated from Lark's blond hair. She wore blue jeans and a red T-shirt. Well, at least the color was good. "I must be binocular-challenged."

"Want some help?"

Rachel handed her the glasses.

"This is the main focus." Lark pointed to the knob on the top of the binoculars, then she gestured to a small knob on the right eyepiece. "This is the diopter knob. It's the fine-tuner, and the last person using these things must have been blind." She twisted the knob counterclockwise. "Okay, now hold the binoculars up to your face and adjust the width of the barrels to fit your eyes. You want to see everything through one big circle, not two."

Rachel took the binoculars and followed Lark's instructions. "Done."

"Now use the focus on top to focus in on something."

"That's better."

"Wait. Now close your left eye and turn the diopter until the image you see through your right eye is clear."

Rachel twisted the eyepiece knob and the Twin Owls buttresses came more sharply into view.

"Clear?" Lark asked.

"Crystal."

"Good." Lark fidgeted, then pointed at the binoculars. "By the way, there's a gauge on the diopter. Make a note of the setting. That way, if someone else uses your binos, you can reset them easy."

Rachel checked. The gauge was numbered clockwise, and the mark fell between the 0 and the 1. "Duly noted. Thanks."

"No problem."

The silence stretched between them until finally Rachel lowered the binoculars. She might as well be the one to broach the subject. "Why didn't you tell me Bursau was staying at The Drummond?"

Lark's chin jutted into the air. "I don't see how it makes any difference."

"It probably doesn't." Rachel turned away and lifted the binoculars back to her eyes. "It's more a matter of trust." Miriam was missing, and Lark had withheld information. Any tidbit, any clue, seemed important, as attested to by the present lawn chair observation.

"I guess I should have coughed it up." Lark crossed her legs and sat down Indian-style on the ground beside the chair. "By the time it seemed relevant, there wasn't much point in bringing it up. The Sheriff's Department had searched the hotel room while you were with Harry in Garcia's car. Anyway, the maid had already cleaned the room, and Garcia's guys found squat."

"How about the maid? Did she tell you she found anything?" Rachel already knew from the interview that she'd told the Gazette reporter the room was empty.

"She claims it was clean."

Rachel refocused the binoculars on the Lower Owl, a small, broken outcrop sitting directly in front of the Twin Owls. Less imposing, the Lower Owl was about half the size of the twin buttresses, a giant mass of gray, craggy rock rising over a hundred feet in the air.

"What are you doing, anyway?" Lark asked, twisting her braid.

Rachel first filled her in on the break-in. "But then I remembered having seen two birds the night we found Bursau's body—the LeConte's sparrow and a raven. Of course, everyone thinks I've lost my mind." She continued to scan the skies. "But Harry helped me find the records on the raven, and I'm trying to find its nest."

"Where is it supposed to be?"

"Do you see that overhang on the southeast side, about three-quarters of the way up?" Rachel pointed. "That's where Eric has the nest marked in his notes." She handed the paper to Lark. "But I can't see it."

"You need to be closer." Lark waggled the paper in front of Rachel's face. "Regardless, you're nuts."

"Ah, you're in the majority."

Lark picked up a pine needle and threw it like a spear at a sprig of red Indian paintbrush. "What are you planning to do if you do spot the bird?"

"Check the nest for something it might have carried off."

"Like a computer disk?"

"I always said you were smart."

"But you can't. Lumpy Ridge is off-limits to climbers, and that includes the Lower Owl. They'll put you in jail if they catch you up there."

"Yeah, if I go to Garcia and he refuses to check out the nest, then I can't climb because he'll know what I'm planning to do. But this way, we'll have the element of surprise on our side, and maybe we won't get caught."

"We?"

Rachel refused to be deterred. "You do know how to climb, don't you?"

Lark hooted. "You're not just crazy, you're certifiable. I'm not going anywhere near that rock."

Rachel's fingers squeezed the binoculars. Roger had taken her climbing once or twice, even if it was under duress. She knew how to look for hand- and footholds, and how to belay. "Well, I am."

"It's too dangerous."

Rachel forced her fingers to relax, lifted the binoculars, and panned the rock face. "I'm not so sure Lower Owl isn't climbable without ropes."

"Right, and Rowdy was a gentle mule."

Rachel grinned at Lark's reference to a past fiasco that had her name written on it. "That was fifteen years ago, Lark."

"My tailbone doesn't remember it that way."

Rachel had dared her to climb on a mule that Uncle William was boarding in a pasture near the barn. "He didn't buck you off until you kicked him."

"That's how you get a horse to move."

"He was a mule."

"I broke my tush."

Rachel laughed. "I'm just glad Uncle William didn't break mine to match. Anyway, this isn't the same." The more she studied the Lower Owl formation, the more convinced she was she could climb the rock, with or without help.

Suddenly, something black moved against the cliff. A bird hopped twice, then rose from a crack on the Lower Owl.

"There it is." She pointed. "Do you see it?"

The bird floated on the thermals, swooping and soaring; a lone, raspy kaw echoed softly from the rocks, breaking the stillness.

"Let me have the binoculars."

"It came from that crack on the right side of the rock."

"What crack? I see fifty cracks."

"No, this one's obvious. You see the Lower Owl formation?"

"Duh."

"Follow a line parallel to the top and join the bottom of the vee, making a triangle. There's a hole on that line, about two-thirds of the way across, that looks like a cave. Imagine it's the pom-pom on a clown's hat. The brim of the hat is the crevice the bird flew out of."

Lark burst out laughing.

"Just shut up and try it." Rachel watched Lark scan the cliff face. She stopped panning, swung the binoculars back, and moved her gaze down a fraction.

"I think I've got it."

"Now all we have to do is climb up there and—"

"I already told you, I'm not going up there. I don't do heights."

"Lark, it's dangerous to climb alone, and Eric's nowhere around. Harry's in Boulder. That leaves the other EPOCH members, and I can't picture Gertie climbing up there."

Lark grinned, then pulled her mouth into a hard line. "The mountain is off-limits for a reason."

"But this could be the clue we need to find Aunt Miriam."

"What about the peregrines and golden eagles? They have nests on the buttresses. If we disturb them, they might abandon their young."

"Then we'll be careful." Rachel pushed herself out of the chair. "Fine, if you won't go with me, I'll go by myself."

"What about EPOCH ethics? You took an oath when you joined the group."

"Aunt Miriam signed me up." Rachel held up her right hand. "I swear, if we see any nesting peregrines, we'll steer clear, go the other way. Besides, Harry told me most of the birds have fledged."

Rachel started to walk away. Lark grabbed her arm. "Everyone in Elk Park can see Twin Owls. We'll be arrested before we can climb halfway to that crack, provided we don't fall and kill ourselves first."

"We don't have to climb to the top, only partway. That section can be seen by only half of Elk Park. Besides, we'll be back down before anyone notices."

Lark pinched her lips together and twisted her braid. Rachel sensed she was wearing down.

"You said you'd teach me things."

"I meant about birding, not playing mountain goat." Lark flipped her braid off her shoulder. "I must be out of my mind, letting you talk me into this. Let's go before I chicken out."

"I knew I could count on you." Rachel clambered out of her chair and clapped Lark on the shoulder. "I'll meet you beside your car in two minutes."

She scooted into the house before Lark reconsidered, grabbed two water bottles, and changed into the hiking boots she'd worn on the last trip she'd taken with Roger. The one to Yellowstone. Lark was leaning against her car when Rachel charged down the front steps a few minutes later. "Ready?"

"As ready as I'll ever be," Lark said, slipping a coil of rope over her shoulder and pointing the way to the start of the trailhead. "I figure we might need it."

Rachel pushed ahead up the short, steep section to the base of the Lower Owl. She knew they were taking a risk. But what other way was there? The longer Aunt Miriam was missing, the less chance they would find her unharmed. Rachel was just relieved Lark had agreed to come along.

The first section was a relatively easy climb along a ridge of trees that angled up the base of the rock. Rachel stumbled once, grabbing a branch for support. The rough bark scraped her hand, and gummy pine sap smeared her fingers.

Soon the trees grew closer together. Rocks cropped up on the downhill side and the cliff face rose sharply on the other, forming a trough that grew steeper with each footstep. The sun beat down on them. Heat rose in waves off the granite rocks.

Rachel stopped as the ground leveled off and flapped her shirttail, cooling her sticky back. She glanced at her watch. They'd been climbing an hour. "This isn't so bad."

"How much further do we have to go?" The tremor in Lark's voice revealed her anxiety. She threw herself against a large boulder, pulled long on her water, and wiped her mouth on her shirtsleeve.

"I think this is where we cut up." Rachel pointed toward a lone tree growing fifty feet above them. "I remember that tree. Another fifty feet above that is the ledge where I spotted the raven."

"You've got to be kidding."

Rachel had grown up in the city, but she'd climbed rocks in the park and on vacations. "Didn't you ever climb rocks as a kid? I'll race you to the tree."

"Lead on, oh fearless one."

Rachel pulled herself up the first boulder, aware that from here on out, they could be seen by anyone in east Elk Park. She had worn a beige shirt and tan jeans, hoping to blend in, but her red hair flamed against the rocks. A dead giveaway. Add that to Lark's bright T-shirt and blue Levis—invisibility was something they had not. "Try and stick to the crevasses wherever possible."

It took nearly another hour to reach the lone tree. Rachel threw herself on the ground, and watched Lark struggle the last five feet. Elk Park stretched out below them, the lake shimmering in the distance. The Drummond Hotel loomed on the ridge, and downtown bustled with life. The summer onslaught of tourists had begun. Let's hope they're all too busy to look up.

Lark crested the ledge, stuck out her tongue, and panted. "And I thought I was in pretty good shape."

"Not!" The muscles in Rachel's calves cramped from exertion, and her arms ached from pulling against the rock. Even working out three times a week on the stair-stepper at the gym hadn't prepared her for this. Still, she liked the heightened senses that came with exhilaration, and the view. She now understood what Roger saw in the sport. "But we're almost there. We can do this."

Her companion eyed the cliff above them dubiously. "That's pretty steep, Rae. More like a technical climb. I think we should turn back."

"Not now that we're this close." Doing something to help find Aunt Miriam had assuaged her worry, if only temporarily. Besides, they'd come too far to give up.

"How are we supposed to get up there?"

Rachel studied the rock, sighting the ledge. The raven swooped in, something gripped in its beak. A few moments later it flapped away. "He looks bigger up close."

"They're known to protect their nests, you know."

"Don't even think you're going to dissuade me."

"Then I'll follow."

"Great." Rachel gripped a knobby chunk of rock, wedged her toe into a knee-high crevice, and reached up. Hand over hand she climbed, the rock biting into her fingers, scraping her knuckles raw. She glanced down once to check on Lark, and the ground wavered below her. The cliff tilted. Rachel closed her eyes and held on.

"What I want to know," called Lark, "is how are we going to get down?"

Rachel pressed her face to the rock, clenched her eyes shut, and pondered the question. Climbing up was one thing; climbing down was another. Going up, she could see where to place her hands and feet, and she didn't have to look at the ground. "Carefully?"

"We're going to die."

"Stop it, Lark." Panicking now served no good purpose. Rachel was already terrified. "We're almost there. Just a few more feet to go."

"I'll wait for you here."

Rachel opened her eyes. The ground steadied, and she could see Lark clinging to a ledge halfway between herself and the lower ledge. Lark's fingers gripped the rock so tightly her knuckles appeared as white as her face.

A loud crack above her made Rachel look up. A rock dropped from the sky. She startled and her foot slipped. Rachel flinched as the rock glanced off the upper ledge. Then she struggled to regain her foothold. The rock tumbled past, crashing to the canyon floor.

Lark shouted, her voice laced with panic. "What was that?"

"A rock. It must have broken loose."

Another crack, and a larger rock careened toward them. Rachel managed to maintain her precarious hold with one hand and cover her head. She lurched sideways as the rock rolled toward her with gathering momentum. Air swished as the rock whizzed past.

Lark stared up from below, her eyes wide with fright. The rock glanced off her fingers, grazing the side of her head. She slumped, pitched backward, and fell. Lark flipped once in the air, slammed against the rock wall, and landed face down on the ground with a sickening thud.

Oh my God! "Lark? Are you okay? Lark, talk to me." Rachel started down the cliff.

Lark moaned and stirred.

Thank God, at least she hadn't broken her neck.

The cliff face seemed steeper and the cracks fewer as she was going down. Rachel groped for a foothold, found a small fissure, and jammed the toe of her boot inside. She stretched, her fingers searching the rock for someplace to grip. "I'm coming, Lark. Say something. Talk to me."

"My leg hurts."

Rachel jumped the last ten feet, landing with a thud inches from where her friend lay crumpled on the ground. A quick assessment confirmed that, aside from a possible concussion, the worst damage was to Lark's right ankle, which was twisted at an odd angle.

A flash of movement overhead caught at the corner of Rachel's eye. Her head snapped up. Another rock? A man dangled from the end of a rope at the edge of the raven's ledge. Climbers! They must have kicked the rocks loose above them.

"Hey, we need some help down here."

The man shrugged and swung onto the ledge. A few minutes later he reappeared, a black square held aloft in his hand.

Adrenalin surged through Rachel's veins. The air crackled with a dry heat. The man wasn't just a climber. He had come here for the computer disk, bombarding them with rocks to keep them at bay. But how had he gotten onto the rocks above them? More to the point, how had he known where to look?

Cold fear coursed through her. Besides Lark and herself, only five people knew about the raven: Eric, Charles, Forest, Harry, and the sheriff. One of them had to have sent the man after the disk.

Rachel squinted up, taking in the man's features: medium height, muscular, jet black hair, a large hooked nose, skin tanned a deep brown. Rachel had never seen him before.

He positioned himself on the ledge, then signaled to someone above him. A second person started down while the stranger picked up a rock, hurling it off the ledge. Rachel dodged. The rock landed just inches from Lark's head.

Raaa-ra. The raven soared into view, then stooped, making a swift line for the man on the ledge. It jabbed its beak toward the man's face, then twisted, flashing its talons.

"Hey! What the—" The man flung up his arms. The disk flew from his grasp, ricocheted, and clattered down the cliff face, landing on a small ledge west of Rachel and Lark.

The raven dived again.

The man she'd now dubbed Igor hollered. His voice, low and harsh, rumbled off the rocks. The other man on the rope lowered himself into kicking range, and swiped at the large black bird.

This was Rachel's chance.

Raaa-ra.

The raven swept in, and Rachel moved quickly. She scrambled to the edge of the ledge, lay on her stomach, and stretched her arm toward the disk. Her fingertips nudged the black square, and it slipped further from reach.

Damn!

A barrage of rocks rained down, and Rachel covered her head. Behind her, Lark curled into the fetal position. Rachel wormed her way forward, leaning out over the ledge. She had almost had it. Her fingertips brushed the disk again, but this time she was able to coax it forward, capturing it in her hand. "Yes!"

"Hey, bitch!"

She glanced up. The raven circled overhead. The men glared down from the upper ledge. "That belongs to my boss," yelled Igor.

"Not anymore." She jammed the disk into her back pocket, and sprinted back to Lark. In a low voice she urged her friend to move. "We have to go. Now! We have to climb down."

"I can't."

"You don't have a choice here."

Igor lowered himself over the ledge.

She had to think fast. Breaking a long branch off the scraggly tree, Rachel snapped it in two. Then, pulling off her belt, she used it and the branches to splint Lark's leg. Thank God for first-aid classes.

Grabbing the rope Lark had brought with them, Rachel looped it around Lark's torso and tied it with a triple knot under her arms. Then she wrapped the free end around the tree and knotted it securely. "How long is the rope, Lark?"

"I don't know."

"Make a guess." She needed one length to lower Lark down—enough to reach from the top of the cliff to the bottom. Twice that to belay herself afterwards.

"Seventy-five feet."

"Long enough."

Rachel prodded Lark. The woman moaned, lolling her head from side to side. Rachel splashed water from one of the bottles into her face, and Lark sputtered out of her pain-induced fog. "Hey!"

"Listen to me. Do you see those two men?"

Igor was nearly halfway down the cliff face, headed straight for them.

"They were the ones throwing rocks," Rachel said. "We have to go. Now! Crawl over to the edge, and I'll let you down."

"It hurts too much."

"Bite on a stick or something." Rachel pinned Lark with a stare. "This is the only choice. You can't climb, and we can't stay here. The tree will work for leverage, but only if we hurry. Otherwise, if Igor and Frankenstein reach us first, Garcia and his buddies are apt to find us both dead at the bottom of the cliff."

Lark registered, and pushed herself up. Pain contorted her face as she pulled herself toward the steep edge.

Rachel checked on Igor's progress. He was within twenty-five feet of the ledge.

"Keep moving, Lark. You're almost there. Good! Now use your good foot to keep yourself away from the rocks."

Lark pulled herself to the cliff and swung her feet out into the air. "I got it."

"Go." Rachel pushed Lark off the edge and leaned on the free end of the rope the way she'd seen Roger do any number of times. Only he had used pitons and carabiners to hold the weight. Rachel used the tree. More primitive, but it worked. In only a minute or two, Lark had reached the ground and collapsed in a heap.

"Untie the rope, Lark. Pull it free from around your waist."

"It hurts too much to move anymore." Tears edged Lark's voice toward hysteria.

"You have to. Please, Lark. Now!"

Lark mustered her reserves and fumbled the knot free, struggling to push herself up. Rachel yanked on the rope, and it wrenched free. She reeled it back up the cliff.

Above her the sounds of Igor kicking rock grew closer. Quickly she looped the rope around herself, then around the tree. Holding onto the loose end of the rope, she drew a deep breath, and stepped off the ledge.

Hand over hand Rachel let out the rope, belaying herself down the craggy cliff. Hemp bit into her palms, and she struggled to control her descent as granite and pine tore at the fibers of the rope. Her boots scuffed the surface of the rock, leaving black marks.

Twenty feet from the bottom, she ran out of rope. As she was holding her weight on the doubled length of line, she heard feet pounding on dirt. Igor was on the ledge.

Spotting a handhold two feet over, Rachel pushed herself sideways toward the fissure. She reached out, managed to grab a handful of rock, and pulled herself tight against the cliff face, jamming her left foot into a thin crack. Secured, she let go of the free end of the rope and sharply tugged on the length still tied around her waist. The free end of rope snaked upward, over the rock above her. A pair of hands reached out. The rope swished through his fingers, back down past her and coiled just below her at the base of the cliff.

"Bitch!" The man above her kicked a rain of dirt onto her head. "Dammit, she's getting away," he called to Frankenstein above him. "Hurry up and get down here with that rope."

Rachel leaped to the ground and gathered the rope in a messy coil, as Igor watched from the ledge. "Come on, Lark. Get on your feet. We may have time if we hurry."

"We'll never make it."

She was right. An experienced climber could descend much faster than she and Lark had, and there was no way Lark could travel quickly with an injured ankle.

"Let's get around the corner," Rachel said softly, "then maybe we can hide."

Lark stared at her in alarm. "What if they find us?"

"Well, if we stay here, they'll find us for sure."

Chapter 12

Rachel heard the men shouting to one another on the ledge. Time was running out. Bracing Lark, she offered her shoulder as a crutch. Lark hobbled forward, gasping in pain.

"Just a little farther," coaxed Rachel. Up ahead she could see a break in the rocks. "You should be able to get over the edge up there."

"Maybe you should just run for help."

"And let those cowboys get their hands on you? I don't think so. I'll use my self-defense training first." Rachel spoke with more bravado than she felt, murmuring encouragement as she secured the rope around Lark for the second time, and helped boost her onto the rocks. "Now swing your legs over the edge, and pivot around on your butt."

Rachel scanned for something to use as a pulley. The nearest tree was too far away, and without leverage she'd never be able to hold Lark's weight. Her gaze caught a sharp spear of rock that jutted up from the ground several feet to her right. Kicking the granite, she pushed against it hard with the flat of her foot. It didn't budge. Looping the loose end of the rope around the stone, she flashed a signal. Lark bit her lip, pushed off and dropped over the edge.

"Move left," she heard Frankenstein yell to Igor. "You're almost down."

Rachel craned her neck to check Lark's progress. The rope, stressed from its earlier use, frayed as it played across the sharp edge of the rock. Please don't let the darn thing snap.

"Are you getting anywhere close to the ground?" she whispered, working to keep the strain from her voice.

"It's still too far down," answered Lark. "But there's a ledge about three feet below me."

"Can you get to it?"

"I can try."

The rope jerked. Rachel tightened her grip. What was Lark doing?

"I've almost got it. A little more." The sound of skittering stones filtered up from below. "Okay, I'm on." Lark moaned. The line fell slack.

Rachel crawled onto the overhang and peered over. A sheer rock face dropped away below her. "I can't see you at all. Wave your hand."

Thirty feet below, Lark's hand jutted out from the granite wall. Rachel tried spotting her from several angles; the ledge remained invisible.

"Can you see anything below you?" Rachel asked.

"Trees. I can't see the ground at all."

"Good. Stay there. Be quiet! I'll be back."

"Rae!"

"Shhhh. You'll be okay. I'm going for help." Rachel dropped the free end of the rope over the edge, and prayed Lark would reel it in.

"I'm down," shouted Igor as Rachel leaped back onto the path.

"Then go get them," shouted the other man. "With that one injured, they couldn't have gone far."

Rachel ran, stumbling on the rocky ground. Branches tore at her arms and face, and scratched her skin. Footsteps pounded behind her, vibrating through the ground as they gathered momentum.

She picked up her speed, sucking in gulps of dusty air, her lungs burning. A cloud of thick brown dust billowed around her feet.

The steep incline caught her unaware. She stumbled over an exposed tree root and fell, skinning her knees and hands. Rachel scrambled back onto her feet, hearing Igor above her. Ignoring the blood trickling down her leg, she sprinted toward the trailhead. The pebbles under her feet rolled like marbles, causing her to lurch.

Igor gained on her, his hands reaching out to prevent her escape. She dodged to the right around a tree in the middle of the path, pouring on extra steam. She heard a crunch and figured Igor must have hit the trunk. With luck it bought her just enough time.

Go. Go.

At a dead run, she rounded the bend. Bird Haven rose in the distance, and there were people milling around the Raptor House. "Help!" she screamed. "Help!"

Several looked up with startled expressions. Eric was just pulling into the lot.

Rachel ran down the access road and made a beeline for his truck. "Eric!"

The ranger jerked his head around, slammed on the brakes, and leaped out of his truck. "What is it? What's wrong?"

Rachel closed the distance between them, afraid to look back. Reaching his side, she grabbed his arm and pointed toward the Lower Owl. Then she doubled over, clasping the stitch in her side, glancing behind her. No one was there.

Eric bent down, and placed a warm and reassuring hand against her back. "What happened? What's going on?"

A man stepped over and joined them. "Is she okay? Are you okay, lady?"

"No. I mean, yes, I'm fine, but Lark's hurt." Rachel pulled several deep breaths and exhaled, then moved away from Eric's touch. What if he was the one who had sent the men after the disk?

More people gathered, and Rachel straightened up. Lark was in trouble. Even if it was Eric, there was nothing he could do with so many witnesses around. "Lark's injured her ankle. We need help up on the Lower Owl."

It took Mountain Search and Rescue several hours to get Lark off the mountain. They used a litter to haul her from her perch on the ledge.

The clinic took several more hours to X-ray and cast her ankle. Two minor breaks. Six weeks in fiberglass. The doctor called her "fortunate."

Sheriff Garcia had been notified by Search and Rescue, so Rachel had been forced to explain Lark's predicament on the ledge. "You didn't take me seriously."

"What the hell were you thinking?" he demanded. "You need to leave the investigating to me."

"Yes, but—"

"No buts about it. I should be slapping your butt in jail." Fortunately, he hadn't, and Eric had driven the two women back to Lark's house.

Watching her friend wince in pain, Rachel squelched the guilt she felt over Lark's injuries and settled a pillow under her leg. "It could have been worse."

"How so?" Lark asked.

"We could have been arrested." Rachel repositioned the ice pack draped across Lark's ankle, and turned up the heat. The Drummond Hotel complex had been built in 1909. It included a concert hall, eighteen-hole golf course, septic system, steam powered generator bank, and thirty-two-room Manor House, known as the "winter hotel." The carriage house, where Lark lived, had served as the Drummonds' personal residence. It seemed Mrs. Drummond was a writer who required privacy for her "artistic endeavors."

According to Aunt Miriam, James Drummond had spent over half a million dollars building the complex, a lot of money in those days. A lot of money today. He should have spent more on caulking.

Lark drew a comforter across her body and shivered. "Guess we're lucky to know a park ranger."

"Lucky," echoed Rachel.

Eric had gotten them off the hook with Garcia by pointing out that the park restrictions for climbers were being lifted on the Lower Owl tomorrow. And that although technically she and Lark were in violation of park regulations, it seemed a waste of time to press charges. For her part, Rachel had written a large check to Mountain Search and Rescue. The sheriff had grumbled a warning and left.

"You know, Rae, you don't have to stay if you don't want to. I'll be fine." Lark's slurred speech signaled that the pain medication prescribed by the doctor was taking effect.

"After I've scoped out the guest bed?" And locked all the doors and windows?

Lark dozed off, and Rachel fingered the disk in her back pocket. Garcia had never asked about it, and she hadn't volunteered. She wanted to know what was on the disk and make a copy before turning it over to the Sheriff's Department.

Lark's home office came fully equipped with a computer, and Rachel flipped it on. The disk was in bad shape. Its plastic casing was creased and punctured, courtesy of the raven or the fall down Lower Owl. The metal end was pulled slightly loose, but the rest looked okay. Rachel pushed the end piece back into place, and slipped the disk into Drive A.

Here goes.

The computer whirred. She clicked the mouse, and the program menu flashed across the screen.

So far, so good.

Using Windows Explorer, she scanned the files. The disk held three pictures and several Word documents. She clicked op one of the pictures and was asked what program to use to open it. After she selected iPhoto Plus, the message Unable to open files using LZW compression popped up. Darn! She'd have to wait until she could open it in Adobe Photoshop on the Macintosh at Bird Haven. Maybe she'd have better luck with the documents.

She opened the folder marked Tanager and viewed the files. There was one marked Opfalc, one marked Will, and one marked Newleads. Rachel tried opening one in WordPerfect and received the message <unknown conversion>.

What other programs did this machine have on it? She scanned the icons on the screen. Microsoft Publisher.

Opening the program, she realized it was a simplified version of Quark. Not only that, it walked you through the process of setting up a document step by step. She choose the option for a blank page and drew in a text box, using the toolbar displayed on the lefthand side of the screen. Under Insert, she found a command that said Text File. Clicking on the command, she typed in a:\Opfalc. Words flowed onto the screen. Yes.

Rachel repeated the process for the other two files and hit Print, then carried the papers back out to the living room. Two hours later, she set down the final page of the Newleads printout and rubbed her eyes.

"Learn anything?" Lark was watching her from the easy chair.

"Only that your theory about Johnson may be right," Rachel

said. "Bursau had three folders of documents and three pictures on the disk. I can't access the photos, but I did finally figure out how to print the files."

"Anything new?"

Rachel handed the printouts to Lark. "The sections titled Opfalc and Will contained information I already knew. Opfalc detailed Operation Falcon, and was essentially a repeat of Bursau's published article on the sting operation. Will was a complete biography of Uncle William. It covers his childhood, education, marriage, and career highlights, like the article in the Elk Park Gazette. Newleads is meatier. It covers the angles."

"I can't read," Lark said, shoving the papers away. "This medicine is making me feel sick."

"Want something to drink? Maybe a soda?"

"Sure."

Rachel got up and poured them both a cola. "According to Bursau's notes, Uncle William supervised a program studying the effects of DDT on peregrine falcons starting in 1978. I guess DDT and DDE, a byproduct of DDT, accumulate in the peregrine."

"That's right. They cause abnormal breeding behavior and thin-shelled eggs, which reduces hatching success." Lark took a drink, set her glass down on the table beside her, and fidgeted with the blanket covering her legs. "But the United States restricted the use of DDT in 1969."

"And Canada did in 1972," Rachel said. "But apparently analysis of unhatched eggs in the seventies and eighties still showed high levels of DDE present."

"That's because of exposure during migration. Heck, they're still using DDT in some Central and South American countries."

"Anyway, Uncle William's research focused on the declining population of peregrines in Rocky Mountain National Park. Research team members spent two-week periods in a cabin within the park boundaries, locating active nests. The number of successful nests was documented and unhatched eggs from failed nests were analyzed for DDE levels."

"So?"

"Apparently, records from 1982 indicated that two eyasses were orphaned and taken back to the university lab for care and feeding. The young falcons thrived, but then, shortly before they were ready to fledge, they mysteriously "died." Uncle William properly documented disposal of the bodies."

"But Bursau didn't think so?"

"No. According to his theory, Uncle William sold the birds to an Arab falconer through an intermediary."

"Who?"

"The notes don't say. There're references to someone named Raven, who's alleged to have initiated contact with the Middle Eastern buyer. Bursau also mentions pictures he'd obtained to substantiate his claim."

"He doesn't say anything else about this intermediary?"

"No," Rachel said, flipping through the papers in her lap. "He just refers to him as someone with 'local ties and foreign contacts.'"

"That fits Mike Johnson," Lark said. "And he's just the type of scum who would sic those goons on us today."

Rachel's throat went dry. "But how would he have known to send someone? The only people who knew about my raven theory besides us were Eric, Harry, Charles, Forest, and Sheriff Garcia."

Lark turned around in her chair. "There's no way Eric or Harry is involved. I'll vouch for both of them, one hundred percent."

"How can you be so sure? Personally, I don't want to suspect any of them. But someone ordered those men to go up on the Lower Owl."

"I'm telling you, look at the others."

Lark was so adamant, Rachel decided not to argue. She'd explore them as possibilities on her own. "Fine. That leaves Charles and Forest... and the sheriff."

"Well, it's obvious Victor's out."

"Why?" Logically Rachel knew Lark was right, but she might as well play devil's advocate. "He seems awfully vested in pinning the rap on Aunt Miriam. Maybe he's trying to cover his own rear end."

"All Vic Garcia ever wanted to be from the time he graduated from high school was a cop."

"How do you know that?"

"Esther Mills, the owner of the Warbler Café, told me. She's his girlfriend. Apparently he started coming up here from Denver with his Big Brother, one of those police officers who volunteer to buddy up with troubled kids. You know, the bad kid—good role model drill. Anyway, it took on Vic."

"What did he do bad?" Not that it mattered, but by now Rachel was curious.

"According to Esther, nothing. He just had the potential. Apparently he saw his uncle shoot and kill his father when he was sixteen, then had to help raise seven brothers and sisters. He used to get a little wild on his days off. Guess his Big Brother straightened him out."

"You said he came up from Denver? How long has he lived up here?"

"Twenty years? I'm guessing, but I'm sure I'm close. I know he was up here in eighty-four because I heard he'd volunteered to go undercover for the U.S. Fish and Wildlife Service during Operation Falcon. They turned him down because he was too well known among the locals."

Rachel rifled the papers. "Did Esther tell you that, too?"

The question hung in the air between them. Finally Lark pulled her braid across her neck and studied the split ends. "No. Mike Johnson did."

Rachel raised her head and looked at Lark. "Was he a friend of yours?"

"Yes." She sighed like a woman resigned to an ugly truth. "When I first moved to Elk Park, I dated him for a while. We even talked about getting married. Then one day, in walks Cindy, and it was out with the old, in with the new. The next thing I knew, they'd tied the knot at the Justice of the Peace, and I was just someone he used to know."

Rachel empathized. "Men can be such scum."

"Sometimes." Lark smiled. "Anyway, some of the trials that came out of Operation Falcon were still going or when Mike and I were dating. He told me his take on what happened, and bragged about 'having the right connections.' At the time I was young, naive, and in love. I assumed he meant that he dealt only with legitimate operators. Guess I was wrong."

Rachel cleared her throat. She didn't know what to say. The "right connections" could mean law enforcement. Maybe the sheriff decided to investigate on his own, and then chose to keep the money instead of turning Johnson in. If he was the "key player" Bursau had referred to, he'd have a good reason to kill the reporter, and a good reason to pin the rap on somebody else. Plus, he was there when she remembered the raven.

"What do you know about Charles and Forest?" she asked. "Does either of them have Middle East connections?"

"They both do."

"Seriously?"

"Yeah." Lark took another sip of her cola. "Charles's are through birding. He's the one who set up Miriam's Middle Eastern birding tour."

"Did he have them in the early eighties?"

"I don't know about that, but I know Forest did." Lark pushed herself up in her chair, wincing as her ankle moved across the footrest. "He grew up overseas. His father was assigned to the diplomatic corps in Egypt."

How did Lark know these things? Bursau's notes didn't have any of this information.

"I know because his dad played golf with my father back in Washington, D.C. His family returned to the States when Forest started college at Northwestern."

That's where Uncle William went to school. "Who's your dad?"

Lark paused. "Nathan Drummond."

"The senator from Connecticut?"

Lark nodded curtly. "Anyway, Forest's dad hunted, and he brought Forest out here on vacation. As soon as Forest graduated from college, he moved to Colorado and set up practice. Like most politicians, he's a lawyer."

Lark's father was Nathan Drummond. That explained a lot of things. Why hadn't Rachel remembered that?

"Are you listening, Rae?"

"I'm sorry. I was thinking about your dad. I'd forgotten that he went into politics."

Lark's face tightened.

Better leave it for later. "So how soon after he moved here did Forest run for office?"

"He'd been here a year."

With Lark's answer, Forest Nettleman climbed to the top of Rachel's unknown-third-party list of suspects. "It takes a lot of money to launch a politician."

"But why would he risk a fledgling career?"

"To fund a fledgling campaign."

Lark scrunched and unscrunched the edge of her blanket. "But he's too much the environmentalist. And he's been that way forever. I remember hearing my father talk about Forest's dad having to bail him out of jail for some act of environmental sabotage while he was in school."

"They call it 'monkey wrenching.' That's something a pro-environment politician might want to keep quiet." Rachel stood up and paced the edge of the Navajo rug. "Did you ever read a novel by Edward Abbey called The Monkey Wrench Gang? It was published in 1975, and was the first definitive book about ecodefense."

"Maybe. What about it?"

"When I was in college, I did a paper on the movements it spawned. A lot of environmental groups organized after the book's publication, specifically one called Earth First!"

"So?"

"So those groups became too mainstream for some members, and several splinter groups formed. For instance, the Earth Liberation Front, the group that claimed responsibility for the fires at Vail, is an offshoot of Earth First! Groups like ELF advocate destruction of property belonging to corporations they believe are hurting the environment. They're covert factions without central organization. In other words, any individual can commit an act of ecoterrorism and claim the action was committed under the umbrella of ELF."

"And your point is…?"

"Have you ever heard of PETE, People for the Ethical

Treatment of the Earth?"

"Sure. They're the group that sent death threats to the vice president for failure to take a tougher stance on environmental issues."

"Right. PETE takes things a step further than ELF, advocating any means necessary to stop the spread of commercialism into the wilderness. In other words, the end always justifies the means."

"I still don't see how that ties in with William and Operation Falcon."

"PETE, unlike ELF, isn't comprised of young people. PETE's comprised of the ecodefense front-runners, older sixties activists who feel the movement never went far enough. Many of them were members of Environmentalists for Earth." Rachel paused. "Didn't you say Forest went to Northwestern University, and that he'd been in trouble there for environmental sabotage?"

"Yeah, for something like that."

"Then he and Uncle William attended the same college, and both were environmental activists."

The women's eyes met.

"So let me get this straight," Lark said. "You're suggesting Forest, as a member of Environmentalists for Earth, was the contact with the Arab, not Mike Johnson?"

"I'm saying it's a possibility."

"Then you're also saying you believe William is guilty as charged."

Rachel glanced at the disk on the coffee table. "I think it's beginning to look that way."

"I don't believe it," Lark said, holding her head in her hands. "Miriam's going to go ballistic. But for the sake of discussion, let's say he was. What's to say he didn't act alone?"

Rachel picked up the disk and waggled it in the air. "Bursau's research indicates third-party involvement."

"So why not Charles?" Lark asked. "I like that better."

"Okay, that's fine with me. He was an old friend of Uncle William's, and from what he said, they'd known each other since they were boys. Do you know where he went to college?"

Lark shook her head. "No, but I don't think he went to Northwestern."

Rachel didn't either. He wore a signet ring, but if she remembered correctly, the setting was square. Uncle William's was large, round, and had a blue stone in the center.

Lark shifted uncomfortably. Rachel pushed aside the papers and checked the ice pack. It was full of water. "Let me get you some more."

While she was plopping ice into the bag, Rachel considered Charles's other possible connections. His views on Johnson's proposed commercial development of the Twin Owls were more in keeping with PETE philosophies than Forest's proposed bill, but she couldn't imagine him dealing with Johnson in the sale of the falcons. It was obvious he hated the man as much as he adored Aunt Miriam.

Lark cringed when Rachel returned and resituated the ice pack on her ankle. Then Rachel fetched a glass of water and two pain pills. "Go back to sleep."

"What are you planning to do with the disk?"

"After I copy it, I guess I'll give it to Garcia."

"You can't."

"Why not? It's proof there was a third party involved in Operation Falcon. Someone with enough at stake to kill Bursau to keep things under wraps."

"Yeah, and Garcia will think it's Miriam."

Rachel stared at Lark. She had been so busy trying to find a way to force Garcia to search for her aunt that she'd missed the obvious. Aunt Miriam's connection to William, her scheduled trip to the Middle East, the missing birds, then her disappearance. The disk information only exacerbated things. "I hadn't thought of that. You might be right."

"Damn straight."

"Except that she wouldn't have known where to look for the disk."

"Unless someone like Charles is feeding her information."

Rachel pondered the idea. What were the options? She could come up with only one. "Then I'll just have to do some investigating myself. I think the first thing I'll do is pay Mike

Johnson a visit."

"You're crazy, Rae. You can't go up there alone. What if he's the killer?"

"Well, I have to do something." She glanced down at the small black disk with its silver square. "If he's the killer, then he knows I have this, right? Which means, if he's got Aunt Miriam, maybe he'll trade."

"Or you become one less problem to eliminate."

Rachel chewed her lower lip. What she really needed was someone to drag out there with her. Lark was out of commission, and in spite of Lark's testimonials, she hesitated to trust Eric or Harry. At least not until she'd had a chance to look into their backgrounds, and check out their possible connections to any of the others. Which left Gertie, Dorothy MacBean, Cecilia Meyer, or Andrew and Opal Henderson.

Or Kirk Udall! She'd almost forgotten about him. She didn't trust him either.

Chapter 13

Rachel slept fitfully, startling at every little noise. Upon rising, the bags under her eyes attested to her lack of sleep. She guzzled a cup of coffee, showered, then telephoned Kirk Udall. He agreed to meet her at the diner on Main Street for breakfast. Better to make her proposition in person.

Traffic was light in downtown Elk Park—a miracle, considering the onslaught of summer tourists Rachel had expected. Main Street looked just as she remembered it—a ten-block stretch lined with brick sidewalks, wooden benches, and shops crammed full of Colorado memorabilia. According to Lark, several million people came from all over the world during the summer season to see the splendors of Rocky Mountain National Park, and eighty-five percent of them stopped in Elk Park to purchase souvenirs.

Rachel parked her car on the street in a spot marked for locals only. The sign, designed to discourage the tourist population from filling every parking spot on Main Street, had been there since Rachel was a teenager, and it reflected local attitude. The town's veneer was one hundred percent cosmopolitan, but underneath, Elk Park was one hundred percent small town. Its residents, as clannish as Scotsmen, spurned the transitory population and distrusted newcomers, of which she was one despite her relationship to Miriam Tanager.

A cabin at the west end of Main Street housed the Elk Park Diner. The hundred-year-old building was constructed of ant-eaten logs and chipped mortar. She pushed open the door to the jingle of bells, and glanced around.

"Over here," called Udall, half-rising from a booth in the smoking section. "I hope you don't mind," he said as Rachel scooted onto the vinyl seat across from him. "This was all they had left."

"It's fine." Rachel reached for a menu and wrinkled her nose at the acrid smell of cigarette smoke that clung to the plastic pages. "How long have you been here?"

She glanced at Udall, and realized he wasn't paying the least bit of attention. His tanned arms rested on the table-top as he leaned forward. His dark eyes scanned the other diners with hungry curiosity.

"Don't you wonder what they do for excitement around here?" he asked.

"They watch the tourists."

A middle-aged waitress in tight jeans approached, clutching a brown plastic carafe. "Coffee?"

"Yes, please. Rachel?"

"Coffee. Black."

The waitress splashed mud-brown liquid into the cup in front of her and took their order. After she'd walked away, Udall fixed Rachel with a hopeful stare. "So, what did you want to see me about, Rachel Stanhope? Have you changed your mind about my offer?"

"I need your help."

"What do I get out of the deal?"

"Always looking for the angle."

His brown eyes studied her face. "You scratch my back…"

"I'll scratch yours," she finished. "I found one of Bursau's disks yesterday."

"You did! Where?"

"Shhhh." She glanced around, pleased to see that none of the other diners seemed to be paying any attention to them. "No one except Lark knows."

"What's on the disk?"

"Interesting stuff." She flashed him a grin. "Willing to bargain?"

He scratched his chin, then pointed at her. "Technically, that disk belongs to Birds of a Feather magazine."

"True, and technically I should have turned it over to Sheriff Garcia. But I didn't. So do you want to make a deal?"

"Fire away."

"I need an escort for dinner tonight."

"What's in it for me?"

"Dinner at one of the most elegant restaurants in Elk Park, and the disk at the end of the night."

He leaned back against the booth, spreading his arms across the back like a bird in flight. "I'm listening."

"I want to go to the Black Canyon Creek Ranch for dinner tonight."

"Mike Johnson's spread?"

She raised her eyebrows. "You've been doing your homework."

"Right on. The Black Canyon Creek Ranch is known for its elegant atmosphere and delicious game meats, and its proprietor is a master falconer with international friends and a taste for fine wine and women."

"Then you'll go?"

"I'm your man. I wouldn't miss it. What time should I pick you up?"

"Make it five-thirty so we'll be in time for cocktails. Dinner at seven."

"Sounds good."

Rachel slipped two dollar bills from her purse and set them on the table. "Oh, and I think it's dressy."

"Then I guess I know how I'm spending the rest of my morning."

The rest of the day went according to plan. With Udall set to make the dinner reservations at Black Canyon Creek Ranch, Rachel had gone back to Bird Haven. After Perky had plucked his daily ration of hair and flown back to his nest, Rachel logged on her computer.

She plugged in the disk, copied the files into a folder, and opened the compressed photograph files. The first two pictures showed William, Forest Nettleman, and a man in a white robe and headdress with two young falcons. The background showed trees, rocks, and ground. Nothing to give a hint as to location.

The most interesting photo, of dubious quality, was the third. It showed an unidentifiable someone opening a briefcase. There was something that seemed familiar, but it was hard to place. Light glinting off metal had burned the negative white in areas, especially around the hands and face, the wrist, and the briefcase handle. But there was no mistaking the contents of the case. They were clear. Bundles of money, and lots of them.

She copied the photo files to the new folder on her computer, then popped the disk out of the A-drive and stuffed it into her purse. She finished the morning by calling all of the EPOCH members to let them know that the Monday afternoon meeting would be canceled because of Lark's injuries and Miriam's disappearance.

Throughout the afternoon, she handled several client matters for Jack Jaffery, then did a web search for information relating to aspects of Miriam's disappearance. She didn't find any new information.

At five o'clock, Rachel logged off and dressed for dinner. About fifteen minutes-later the phone rang.

"Hello?"

"Rachel, Kirk here."

She glanced at her watch. "Where are you?"

"I got hung up, and I may have to bag out early. My boss called. There are problems with another story. Any chance you could meet me up there?"

Rachel hesitated. "Sure. What time?"

"Shoot for half an hour."

Twenty-five minutes later, Rachel pulled onto Black Canyon Creek Ranch Road. The turnoff was just beyond the overhead sign marking the entrance to Bird Haven off of Raptor House Road, and the road cut across a small portion of the southeast corner of Miriam's property. The previous owners had granted Mike Johnson an easement. Now, it seemed, he wanted more than just access to the main road; he wanted access across the property to Twin Owls.

The road rippled with washboard caused by heavy runoff, and the car lurched and bumped, locking the seat belt across her shoulder in jarring fits and starts. She accelerated through a narrow stretch where tall pines jutted skyward, blocking the sun, and slowed again when the drive opened into a bright clearing. A turkey vulture circled high overhead, and in the distance a large bull elk grazed on dry-land shrubs and brightly colored wildflowers.

The ranch house, a meandering two-story structure, sprawled

across the upper reaches of the clearing. Udall, dressed in a coat and tie, waited on the wide porch. "You clean up nice."

"Thanks, I think."

"I can't believe I beat you."

She breathed a sigh. "After jouncing up that road, I'm surprised I made it at all."

He gestured grandly toward the front door. "Well, the bar is this way, and dinner's set for seven."

The lounge was situated in a spacious room finished in white aspen wood. Liquor bottles lined the mirrored wall behind the bar, and a massive stone fireplace sported a stuffed mountain lion poised to spring off its mantel. They were the first guests to arrive. Udall steered her toward a corner table.

"I'll have a vodka martini," he told the waitress.

"That sounds good," Rachel said. "Make mine with three olives, please."

Another couple arrived while they waited for their drinks. The woman, a stately blond, was draped in a full-length sequined gown, spike heels, and fur wrap. The man, whose back was to Rachel, wore a tuxedo.

Rachel glanced down at her black shift and black flats. The combination usually sufficed for New York.

"Don't worry. You look great."

Rachel smiled, and fingered the strand of pearls at her neck. It had been a while since a man had complimented her appearance. She kind of enjoyed it. "Thanks again."

"Ah, Sheikh Al-Fassi. How good to see you."

Rachel's heart pounded as the man speaking stepped from behind the bar and extended his hand. Of average height, average color, and average build, there was nothing remarkable or defining about him. What distinguished him was his deep, resonant voice.

The sheikh turned when the man addressed him, smoothed a jet black mustache, and assessed the man with cool detachment before nodding. "Mr. Johnson."

Was the sheikh the man in the picture? Take away fifteen years and the mustache, and it was a distinct possibility.

"I trust everything's been okay so far?" asked Johnson.

Rachel tried picturing him with Lark. Her "back to basics" lifestyle didn't mesh with his yuppie "me, me, me" demeanor.

"Everything's been fine, thank you." The sheikh gestured to the woman beside him. "Have you met my wife?"

"I don't believe I've had the pleasure." Johnson's eyes raked the woman's body. "How do you do, Mrs. Al-Fassi?"

The woman smiled. Her husband handed her a glass of red wine.

"So, what do you think? You must agree, we have a nice place here." Johnson gestured expansively, his voice vibrating in the air like a sonic boom.

"The accommodations are quite satisfactory," replied the sheikh. "Though, I admit, I'm more anxious to see the birds in use."

"Then tomorrow's your lucky day." Johnson clapped the sheikh on the shoulder.

"Yes." The sheikh brushed off his sleeve. "I'm looking forward to it."

At that precise moment, a commotion erupted in the foyer as a large party entered, making their way toward the lounge. Rachel closed her eyes and strained to hear the conversation between Johnson and the sheikh.

Udall spoke out of the side of his mouth. "Did you invite them?"

"Who?" Rachel opened her eyes, and was shocked to see Eric and Harry entering the room with Gertie, Dorothy, and Cecilia in tow.

"Well, look who's here," chirped Gertie, sidling over to the table.

Udall flashed a smile.

"Don't let her kid you, Rachel," Dorothy said. "She knew you were here."

Gertie dropped her voice. "Lark told us what you were up to."

Rachel had sworn Lark to secrecy. "I guess you can't trust anyone these days."

"Some people just have better judgment than others," Gertie murmured.

"Oh, look, Dorothy," Cecilia said. "Doesn't Mike Johnson

look handsome tonight?"

"Stop it, Cecilia." She looked pointedly at her sister. "Quit trying to fix me up. We came up here to help Rachel."

"Lark's afraid you're going to get yourself into trouble," explained Harry.

"Now how would a pretty young lady like this get herself into trouble up here?" asked Mike Johnson, approaching the table.

"We thought you might throw us out, Mike," Eric said. "After all, we are adversaries of a sort."

"Adversity makes for adventure, my good man. And planning makes for perfection."

"Good to see you, Mike." Eric shook his hand. The others followed suit. Harry introduced Kirk Udall, then Rachel as Miriam Tanager's niece.

"I heard about your aunt's disappearance, Ms. Stanhope. I'm very sorry." Johnson wasted no time in finding a diversion. "It looks like they're signaling to me from the kitchen. If you'll excuse me? Enjoy your dinner."

The EPOCH members pulled over another table, drew up chairs and ordered drinks. Eric plopped down beside Rachel and gestured in the direction of the bar. "Forest is here, too. He was surprised to see some friends of his seated over near the bar."

Rachel spotted Forest at a table with the Al-Fassis. The fact they were old friends of his, and staying at Mike Johnson's, seemed to be too much of a coincidence.

"Charles stayed behind with Lark," Cecilia said. "He's guarding her in case one of those thugs from the Lower Owl decides to pay her a visit while we're all up here."

"She told us what happened," Harry said.

"Oh, my, it sounded perfectly awful." Dorothy dropped her voice. "But maybe we shouldn't talk about that here."

"Why not? We need to talk about it sometime," said Gertie, shrugging out of her coat and fluffing her bob. "Lark told us you found one of the disks and that it contained some information about my father. I want it."

"Hey, wait just a minute there," Udall protested. "That disk is Birds of a Feather magazine's property."

"Well, the two of them should have taken it straight to

Victor," Cecilia said.

Rachel sipped her martini.

Gertie crossed her arms. "I always call things as I see them, which is the only reason I'm here. Lark told us what was on that disk. I absolutely refuse to believe that my father was involved in anything shady. Someone's trying to frame him, and I intend to find out who."

Rachel dunked the olives in her martini glass, splashing vodka dots on the cocktail table. "And what about Aunt Miriam, Gertie? Do you believe she's innocent?"

Gertie's color heightened to match her rouge. "If they set up Daddy, they probably set up Miriam, too. You may be right about her being in some sort of danger."

It was about time.

"Who's 'they'?" Cecilia asked.

Dorothy slapped her sister's arm. "That's what we're here to find out. Haven't you been paying any attention?"

The women erupted in battle, picking and pecking at each other like a couple of old hens. Forest made a beeline for their table.

"Ladies!" His stern voice silenced their bickering. He cleared his throat, shooting a warning glance in their direction. "Everyone, I'd like you to meet an old friend of mine, His Highness Sheikh Al-Fassi, and his wife, Elaina. The sheikh and I attended high school together in Riyadh."

"Oh, you've known each other for quite a few years," Dorothy said.

"Thirty-five, to be exact," said the sheikh, bending over her hand. "And you must have been just a youngster back then."

"She was," Cecilia said, winking at Rachel.

The sheikh was a charmer, just like her own soon-to-be ex-husband, and Rachel smiled sympathetically at Elaina Al-Fassi. She seemed oblivious to the attention.

"Please, won't you all join Elaina and me for dinner? Mr. Johnson"—the sheikh waved him from behind the bar—"I want you to reset my table for ten. No, wait, eleven, if you care to join us as well. And another round of drinks while we wait."

Rachel had turned down the drink, but by the time the table

was ready, she was wishing she'd indulged. Gertie had made a competition out of flirting with the sheikh, and Cecilia was pouting. Harry, Eric, Forest, and Kirk spent the time talking birds. Elaina Al-Fassi hadn't said a word.

"I hope you don't mind my selfishness, placing you beside me," the sheikh said when they'd finally been seated for dinner. He pulled out Rachel's chair and spoke softly in her ear. "You're a lovely girl. I've been hoping to have a chance to talk with you over dinner."

The conversation revolved around food. Rachel ordered a Caesar salad, and the sheikh convinced her to try the elk steak smothered in sauted mushrooms.

Mike Johnson preened. "It's a specialty of the house."

Rachel asked for it well done. The sheikh changed her request to medium. "The meat gets tough if you overcook it."

The more time she spent around him, the more he reminded her of Roger. She was quickly losing her appetite.

While everyone ordered, Rachel looked around the dining room. It dripped with elegance. The tables were draped in burgundy and set with sterling silverware. Linen napkins were fanned open on white china plates edged in cranberry and black. Ice and lemon wedges sparkled inside crystal glasses. Three elk horn chandeliers threw muted light from the ceiling, and flickering candles cast seductive shadows across the diners.

"So, Mrs. Stanhope, where are you from?" asked Sheikh Al-Fassi.

"New York City. I work for a marketing firm in Manhattan."

"How interesting. Do you like your job?"

His eyes mesmerized her, so dark they appeared black in the wavering light. "Yes, I do." She told him a little about her work, and about growing up in Chicago. "Where do you live?"

"My wife and I live in Riyadh, Saudi Arabia. Have you ever been there?"

"No." Rachel pleated her napkin. "My aunt was, is, supposed to visit there in a couple of weeks."

"Really?" He turned to Dorothy and Cecilia. "And which one of you lovely ladies is her aunt? Or are you both aunts? Perhaps I should ask which one of you lovely ladies is traveling to my country."

"Oh my, neither. None of the above." Dorothy pulled her head between her shoulders like a frightened turtle. "Miriam's not here."

"Miriam Tanager is the woman I was telling you about, Sheikh," Johnson said, his face as impassive as a piece of granite. "The owner of the Raptor House. She's the one that's missing."

The sheikh nodded. "I'm sorry to hear about your aunt's troubles."

Rachel wondered what Johnson had told him.

There was an awkward lull in the conversation, then Harry spoke. "I've been in Riyadh, I spent almost a year there working on my dissertation. I conducted research on the Houbara bustard."

Rachel's mouth went dry. She reached for her glass of water. Another Middle East connection. But if he was guilty, why reveal himself? Wouldn't he try to keep the information secret?

"What year would that have been?" the sheikh asked.

"Nineteen eighty-six, eighty-seven."

Rachel suppressed an audible sigh of relief. Two years after Operation Falcon. And if his story was true, she ought to be able to verify the dates.

Harry leaned his elbows on the table, his mustard-and-brown Harris tweed sports jacket clashing with the tablecloth. "I actually witnessed a Bedouin flying his birds while I was there."

"And did you enjoy that?"

"Of course, though I don't know much about falconry. Except that it's a sport that seems to have severely depleted the population of bustard."

"Your point is well taken." The sheikh set down his fork and folded his hands. "Falconry is something that goes back to ancient times in my country. My people depended on falcons to hunt meat, supplementing an otherwise meager diet of dates, milk, and bread. It has always been an integral part of desert life."

"And now?"

"It is a great sport, enjoyed by rich and poor alike. It teaches many things—endurance, strength, and patience." The sheikh picked up his fork and speared a piece of lettuce. "And we have come to realize that the survival of falconry depends on the conservation of prey and habitat."

"I overheard you tell Mike that you're anxious to see the birds fly, Your Highness," Rachel said, not yet willing to drop the subject. "Are you planning to go hunting while you're here?"

"Call me Mohammed. And the answer is yes. Tell me, do you like birds, too?"

"I know very little about them." She assumed he meant raptors.

"They are my favorite creature. Mr. Johnson was telling me about the wonderful work your aunt is doing in raptor rehabilitation. I was hoping to be able to see her facility."

"You have asked my husband to talk about his true love," Elaina Al-Fassi said.

"No, my dear, you are my true love. Falconry is only my passion."

"Sheikh, you do realize you're talking to a group of birdwatchers?" Johnson said, setting his napkin on the table and signaling the wine steward. The sheikh looked puzzled.

"He means most of us don't approve of killing birds for sport," Gertie said.

"While I respect your position, Madam, it's more than a sport. It's tradition."

"I'm afraid you'll have to count me a curmudgeon, too, Mohammed," Forest said.

"I'm not sure I understand your disapproval. The meat from the hunt is used either to feed the falcon or to feed the master. It's certainly much more noble than raising chickens."

Chapter 14

Rachel spent a jittery forty-five minutes listening to a lively debate on the merits and history of hunting in society. By the end of the meal, only one thing was clear. The EPOCH members did not approve of owning wild raptors, and the sheikh thought falconry a noble art. They agreed to disagree.

The first opportunity for investigation came as they got up from dinner and Harry broached the subject with Johnson. "I hear you have a nice set of mews, Mike."

"Ja," Eric said. "Any chance we could see them?"

"Tonight?" Johnson acted surprised, but he didn't hesitate. "Anyone interested in a tour, follow me."

Elaina Al-Fassi rose, and all of the men stood up. "If you don't mind, I think I'll go up to my room now."

"It was nice meeting you, Your Highness," Rachel said, unsure what to call a sheikh's wife.

"And you." She bowed her head slightly, then walked around the table for a peck on the cheek from the sheikh.

Rachel ducked into the bathroom before joining the others outside. They had started for the barn ahead of her, but she could still hear their voices as she stepped outside and the wind wrapped itself around her bare arms. She wished she'd remembered a jacket.

As she walked toward the circle of pale yellow light shining through the open barn door, the uneven ground forcing her to slow her usual power-walk pace, Rachel marveled at the brilliance of the moon lighting the path. Stars shone in patterns that she only vaguely remembered from school textbooks, unobscured by the permanent glow of the city.

A pebble sneaked its way into her shoe. She stopped at the end of the porch, leaned against the wooden skirt, and slipped off her shoe. A movement from the ranch house caught her attention. A man – Igor – stepped out on the porch and moved in her direction. He drew long on a cigarette, then Frankenstein joined him. Rachel slipped deeper into the shadows.

"She's here."

"I know," Igor said. "I saw her."

"Did you talk to Raven?"

Raven? That was the name in Bursau's notes, the one used by the middleman in the peregrine sale. And with these goons showing up here, it seemed likely they were connected to Mike Johnson's brigade. Did that mean Johnson had sent them after the disk? Did that make Mike Johnson 'Raven'?

"He said she's harmless. The girl told Raven they got squat off that disk. We're safe for the time being."

Girl? So there was a woman involved.

"Still, I wish this was finished."

"Tomorrow. That's when we send the final message." Igor took another drag of his cigarette, then stubbed it out on the porch.

Hadn't Johnson told the sheikh tomorrow was his lucky day? Did the "final message" mean the birds?

"That's a nasty habit."

"Yeah, well, it's a nervous habit." Igor glanced around as though afraid of being seen, then started down the steps in the direction of the parking lot. "Let's get out of here."

Frankenstein followed, and Rachel debated what to do. She didn't know who Raven was, so going inside the barn to elicit help was out of the question. Getting the license plate number of their vehicle was imperative.

Rachel slipped on her shoe and stepped forward. Gravel crunched under her feet. Igor stopped.

"Did you hear something?"

"No."

"Listen!"

Rachel froze in place, standing on one leg and holding her breath. She felt like a clumsy flamingo, wavering in the dark.

"You always this nervous, boy?" Frankenstein slapped him on the back. "Let's fly."

Rachel exhaled. Pulling off her shoes, she dangled them from her fingers and minced forward in her stockings. The rocks jabbed against the soles of her feet. She looked like an untrained firewalker on hot coals as she moved toward the parking lot.

She crouched low, but stuck to the path to avoid any unfriendly cactus in the dark.

The two men approached a late-model pickup truck, blue with a green-and-white license plate. Colorado. She couldn't read the numbers. Slowly she moved along the row of parked cars separating her from the men.

"Hey!"

Udall's voice boomed from the porch, causing Rachel to jump and the men to turn. Igor cursed.

"Kirk!" Rachel moved to meet him as he walked toward her.

"You weren't planning to sneak out on me?"

"Of course not, I was just going to grab something from the car." She leaned toward him and whispered, "Those are the two men from the cliff."

"Did you get what you needed?"

Had he heard her? She wished she knew what Igor and Frankenstein were up to. Her back was to them now. "Maybe we should join the others."

"That sounds like an excellent idea." He pointed for her to go ahead of him.

Frustrated by her predicament, she avoided looking directly at Igor or the truck. She was still too far away to read the license plate number, but maybe if she steered Kirk closer to the pickup, she'd be able to pick up the numbers.

"Scoot over a row," she murmured, leaning against him to push him sideways.

Udall refused to cooperate. Veering between two cars, he took off toward the barn. Rachel glanced back. Igor stood on the truck's running board. The other man started the pickup. Igor saluted.

Rachel threw down a shoe. "Thanks a lot, Udall. Just what did you think you were doing? I needed to get the license plate number off that truck."

"You should have said something."

"I did."

"Then you should have said it so I could hear you."

I thought I had.

"So what now?" he asked.

"Now, I'm going to catch up to the others."

He reached out and stopped her as she slipped on her shoes. "That's great, but I've got to go."

"You're going to make me walk out to the barn alone after seeing those goons here?"

"Hey, they left." He grinned, and the moonlight bounced off his teeth.

"What about their boss?"

He rubbed his goatee with four fingers, his thumb pressed under his chin. What was it about men and facial hair? They always had to play with it. "I'll watch to make sure you get safely inside. But first, you promised me the disk."

Grudgingly she retrieved it from her purse. "Here. Satisfied?"

"I thank you. My publisher thanks you."

"Yeah, yeah!"

Rachel reached the barn, only to find it empty. A quick look around assured her that there was not much difference between Mike Johnson's accommodations for his birds and the Raptor House's. There was also no sign of either the gyrfalcon or the young peregrines.

Tromping back to the main lodge, Rachel wondered again why Udall was in such a hurry. Did he know something she didn't know? Like where Miriam was? Maybe that was why he dashed off so quickly after dinner.

She expected to find the others in the bar, but there was no one there except the bartender. A few late stragglers were laughing over their dinner in the dining room, but the birdwatcher brigade appeared to have left.

"They've been gone a while," the bartender said. "Most of them split right after the tour."

She scooted out to the parking lot in the dark. The moon had set, and the night sky twinkled with dots of light. The wind whistled through the trees; the shadows swayed across the uneven ground. Every creak from the barn, bang of a shutter, and hoot of a night bird caused her to jump.

Her sense of adventure gave way to jitters as Rachel fumbled for her keys. Her car was one of a handful left in the parking area, and the buildings lay dark. It hadn't taken everyone long to turn out the lights.

Rachel fitted the key in the door, threw her purse on the seat, and, after a cursory search for serial killers, jumped in and threw the lock. The dome light faded to black and she drew a deep breath.

The car fired on the first try, the headlamps lighting automatically. Rachel pulled out of the parking lot. The road seemed bumpier in the dark. She hoped she didn't have a low tire. Maybe she should get out and check. Instead, she drove more slowly, gaining speed in spite of riding the brake. The car lurched as she started down the incline toward the meadow, and she stamped hard on the brakes. The pedal sank to the floor.

What the...? She let off, and depressed the pedal again. Still no resistance. She pumped the brakes and gripped the wheel, watching the front end of the car eat up the road. The seat belt strap locked tight, bruising her shoulder with each bump and jolt.

Rachel stepped on the emergency brake.

Nothing.

She released it and tried again.

Still nothing.

The car was traveling forty-five miles an hour and picking up speed. To bail out would be suicide. To stay with the car seemed certain death.

She hit a pothole and the car careened toward the clearing, headlamp beams sweeping the grass. She yanked the wheel hard, and pulled back onto the road.

What would happen if she turned off the engine? She twisted the key. The power steering failed. Damn! On the steep incline, the car continued to roll, gaining speed. She fought for control and cranked the key. The car engine fired.

That didn't work, but what would happen if she rammed the car into first? The rental car was an automatic. Would downshifting strip the gears and throw the car into neutral? That would make her go faster. But downshifting might give her some engine braking power. There was only one way to find out.

Rachel gripped the shifter, depressed the button on the handle, and yanked back. The indicator needle jumped from third to second to first.

She was still going too fast, but the engine drag helped prevent her from gaining speed too quickly. She jerked the wheel back and forth, keeping the car on the road. The ruts and potholes slowed her course, and she zigged and zagged her way down the hill.

The road leveled out past the clearing before plunging toward Raptor House Road. If her memory served, the trees crowded closer through that stretch. If she maintained control until then, she could jump, or at the very least use the trees to slow her progress.

Either way, she knew she had to do something before that last stretch. Otherwise, she'd end up wrapped around the entrance sign to Bird Haven, swimming in Black Canyon Creek, or communing with an Elk Park telephone pole.

The meadow clearing whipped by. In the rearview mirror, Black Canyon Creek Ranch loomed on the hill. Ahead of her the road pitched down steeply, then leveled off. She aimed the car for the split in the trees.

The speedometer read fifty-five as she shot into the narrow corridor. Fifty-four, fifty-three. When the needle hit forty-five, Rachel realized she needed another plan. In a hundred-feet the road dropped again, sharply.

You need a plan, Stanhope.

She'd seen stunt drivers scrape the side of a car against a building to slow themselves down, but scraping against the trees seemed too risky. A slight miscalculation, a jutting branch, and she'd be testing the air bag. It might come to that yet, but she preferred to stall.

Wait! What if she cleared the end of the trees, then, before the road dropped away, made a sweeping turn back up the hill. That way, when she plowed into the forest, she'd be moving slower.

Rachel braced herself, gripped the wheel, and flipped on the brights as she shot out of the tree-lined corridor. The incline drew closer. Closer. Wait. Wait! Now!

She yanked the wheel hard to the right. The car lurched onto the shoulder of the road. Rocks and brush battered the undercarriage. The ground broke away sharply on her left. She yanked the wheel harder.

Her left front tire hit a rock, and the front of the car bounced in the air. The turning, the momentum, the terrain worked against her. The car started flipping.

Everything slowed.

The front of the car rose in the air, like a breaching whale in slow-motion. The driver's-side window dropped toward the ground, and the terrain fell away like the first hill on the roller coaster at Coney Island.

The car rolled.

Chapter 15

The car came to rest in a pile of rocks, spewing steam from its chassis like a spouting whale. The airbag protected Rachel from the spray of scalding water, and she unclipped her seat belt and tried the door. Jammed. It figured.

There was no power, but the window had shattered when the car landed. She pulled off a shoe, banged out the last shards of glass, and squeezed through the opening, finding a perch on a rock several feet from the car.

Her head hurt. Her shoulder hurt. Otherwise, she seemed to be fine. What had happened?

She remembered trying to turn the car, hitting the rock, and the car flipping. But why hadn't she had any brakes? Someone must have cut the brake lines on her car. But who? Igor?

The night air pierced the thin layer of her black shift, and she shivered. A branch snapped. The car belched. A chill crawled up her spine.

Was someone stalking her in the dark?

She shook off the thought. As far as anyone knew, she had already gone home. Otherwise, wouldn't someone have waited for her?

The first thing she needed to do was call for help. Her cell phone was in her purse, which was in the car. She approached the vehicle cautiously. Steam still hissed from the radiator, and she thought she smelled smoke.

Her purse had fallen to the floor on the passenger's side. She tried the door. Locked. They were all locked, and there was no power. She'd have to go back through the window.

She squeezed through the opening head first and stretched, trying to reach the strap of her handbag. Finally, she crawled inside. Smoke billowed from the engine compartment as she closed her hands on the cell phone. Fire!

She scrambled back across the seat. Broken glass slashed her leg.

Limping a safe distance from the car, she flipped open the cell phone and dialed 911. A message flashed across the digital face of the phone. No Service. She tried again and got the same message.

Flames now lapped at the seats of the car, melting the vinyl interior. Surely someone in Elk Park would see the flames.

Heat from the fire drove her back. Dry brush crackled around the car. She had to go for help.

Rachel stuck to the road, running in spurts. Her head pounded, and the jarring movement sent shooting pains through her shoulder. Her lungs burned from exertion, and the night sounds caused her to keep glancing back over her shoulder.

When she reached Raptor House Road, she faced a dilemma. Did she head for town or for Bird Haven?

Bird Haven perched dark on the knoll. The house blocked the view of the Raptor House from this angle, so she had no way of knowing if any lights shone in the outbuildings. She weighed her options.

If she took off for Elk Park, she was bound to meet emergency equipment on the road, provided someone had spotted and reported the fire. Regardless, there was civilization in that direction.

On the other hand, Bird Haven was closer, and there was a telephone handy.

Either way; she might run into Igor and his friend, or Raven.

She opted for Bird Haven. The road carved through the meadow, and she stuck to the center of the gravel. Stars dotted the sky. An owl hooted. A night creature rustled the grass.

Rachel broke into a sprint as headlights whipped around the curve from Elk Park. The vehicle turned onto Raptor House Road. A pickup!

She dived for the ditch by the side of the road. Thistles pulled at her stockings and dress. Her knee came down on a cactus, the needles jabbing into her skin. The truck turned toward Black Canyon Creek Ranch. Rachel stood up and ran for home.

Bird Haven was locked up tight, and Rachel's keys were dangling from the ignition of the burning car. She tried the front, then the two back, doors. What now? Maybe there was an extra set of keys in the Raptor House. Rachel ran to the barn.

The barn door was open! She slowed. Creeping to the entrance, she peeked inside. A light shone from the office. Eric?

His truck was in the parking lot, but he'd arrived at Black Canyon Creek Ranch with Harry and the others, so it was possible he'd left his vehicle here for the night.

She debated what to do. Eric was still on her suspect list. He knew what car she drove, and where she had been tonight. Yet Rachel's gut told her Forest Nettleman was the one to watch, and Lark had concurred. Time to tempt fate.

She inched forward. What if it wasn't Eric? What if it was—

Eric stepped from the office, a notebook in hand. "Who's there?" He squinted. "Rachel, is that you?"

"Yes. I, ah, do you have a key to the house?"

"Ja, I think so. I believe Miriam keeps one out here in a drawer." He reached for the lights. "Are you okay?"

The lights flashed on, and Rachel heard Eric gasp.

"My God, what happened to you?" He moved quickly toward her.

She glanced down at her torn dress. Cactus needles poked from one knee, and blood caked her legs. Her dress was blood-soaked in spots, covered in dirt and pieces of dried weeds. Her head ached. "I had an accident."

The tears came without warning. Eric stared, then took her arm and steered her toward a chair. "Sit down. Did you call the sheriff?"

Should she tell him the truth, that her stupid cell phone wouldn't work, or should she lie? Neither, she thought, gripped by an anxiety attack. She'd hyperventilate.

"Here," Eric said, grabbing a plastic glove from a box in the veterinarian supply cabinet. "Breathe into this." Then, while she exhaled and inhaled into the glove, he placed a call to Garcia's office.

A sudden calm washed over Rachel. He wasn't the killer. Otherwise, why would he have called the sheriff?

"Feel better?" he asked, as he found the key.

"Much."

"Vic's on his way." Eric walked Rachel over to Bird Haven. She gimped along beside him, grateful for his solid presence, keeping the shadows at bay.

Perky attacked her as they walked in the door.

"Leave me alone!" Another flood of tears made her conclude that she must be in shock.

What's your problem, Chicky Baby?

"Not now, Perky," ordered Eric. He guided her to her room, then stood awkwardly. "Do you need any help?" He glanced down at her knee with the cactus needles sticking out like cloves in an orange. "Can I get you anything?"

She shook her head, bringing on a wave of pain. "I'll be out after I wash up."

"Great," he said, backing out the door. "I'll wait for you in the kitchen."

Coffee was brewing by the time Rachel had showered, cleaned her cuts, and changed. She could smell it as she threaded her way down the hall, through the living room, and into the kitchen. Eric and Sheriff Garcia were drinking coffee in the family room.

"What happened?" Garcia asked with no preliminaries.

Rachel filled him in on the details. She told him about dinner, the sheikh, Igor, and the car accident. She glanced at Eric, and recounted her suspicion that one of the men who knew about her plan to locate the raven was behind the attack. She omitted the part about finding the disk and giving it to Udall, afraid Garcia would arrest her for tampering with evidence in a murder investigation.

"You're lucky you weren't killed. That car's burned so badly it could take days to figure out what made your brakes fail."

"You think?" Eric said. "I'll bet they were cut."

Garcia left, and Eric insisted on camping out in the family room. Secretly, Rachel felt relieved.

"Want some breakfast?" she asked, limping into the kitchen the next morning.

"Ja, but why don't you let me cook? You sit down."

She gratefully accepted, and watched him gather ingredients. "So what brought you to the United States, Eric?"

"Work." He told her about growing up in Norway and his love

for the outdoors. "Norwegians are born to love nature. When I was eighteen, I read about Rocky Mountain National Park in a magazine and decided to come. I fell in love with the wilderness here, enrolled in school, and stayed. I went back to Norway for a short time after I graduated, but there was no work like here. When I came back, your Aunt Miriam and Uncle William agreed to sponsor my citizenship."

"How did you meet them?"

"I took a class from William while I was an undergraduate. Charles taught there, too. He took a sabbatical to do some research work the year I graduated." Eric scooped an omelet onto a plate, garnished it with three strips of bacon, and deposited it in front of Rachel. "Charles and William had a real falling out that year."

"Was Forest living here at the time?"

"Ja. Why?"

"I think Uncle William and Forest were involved in selling peregrines to the Arabs during Operation Falcon."

"No way." Eric stopped what he was doing. "I refuse to believe it." He resumed shoveling an omelet onto his plate. "It's just not possible."

His second assertion didn't sound as emphatic as the first. "Why? You remember something, don't you?"

Eric swallowed, his Adam's apple bobbing in his throat. "The class I took from William was a research class."

"Studying the effects of DDT on peregrines?"

"Ja. How did you know?"

"I found Bursau's notes."

He raised his eyebrows and joined her at the table. "So you know that we found two eyasses abandoned in the park."

Rachel nodded, her heart skipping a beat.

"Right before the birds were scheduled for release, the department decided to keep them for research purposes, then shortly after that, they died. That was the same time that William and Charles had their row. It was also the same time Sheikh Al-Fassi was in Elk Park, visiting Forest Nettleman."

"You're sure of that?"

"Ja." He spread his arms wide. "When you're twenty and

come from a land of kings and queens, you don't forget royal visits. I was quite impressed, even though I didn't meet the sheikh."

"Then it all fits."

"No, nothing fits. All three men were dedicated environmentalists. Not one of them would have sold those birds into a lifetime of captivity."

What Eric said was true. Still, she'd seen the pictures of Uncle William, Forest, and Sheikh Al-Fassi. "I have something to show you."

Rachel lugged her laptop computer into the kitchen. Setting it on the breakfast nook table, she booted it up and inserted the disk. One click and a command to open the file brought up the picture. Eric looked stunned.

"Did you show this to Vic?"

"No. I gave the disk to Udall."

"You did what?"

"We had a deal."

Eric worked his jaw, then finally pounded his fist on the table. "You have to show this to Vic. He's the sheriff. You should have turned the disk over to him."

"I know, but how could I, after keeping it a secret?" She pushed back a stray lock of red hair. "I figure that Udall will share the information as soon as he takes what he wants off the disk. And, other than the photographs, there's nothing there Garcia doesn't already know."

"That's corroborating evidence."

"That substantiates Aunt Miriam's motive."

He rubbed his cheek like he'd been slapped. "Or Gertie's."

"Or mine, or anybody's that might have wanted to protect Uncle William's reputation." Rachel stared at the computer screen. "Let's go back over it in light of this photograph. Bursau claimed that Uncle William sold the birds to an Arab, using an unknown middleman, right?"

Eric nodded.

"And the picture seems to substantiate that fact. Second, William and Charles had a falling out, suggesting that they had disagreed about something, right around the time the eyasses died."

"Ja."

"I say Charles knows more than he's letting on. Maybe it's time we asked him what happened."

Eric scooped up a mouthful of eggs and washed them down with coffee. "I'm beginning to see how this could have come together."

"Didn't you say Charles took a year's sabbatical the semester after the eyasses died?"

"Ja."

"What if Forest negotiated the deal with his friend, Sheikh Al-Fassi, then William says the birds died, and fakes the records." She paused to let the information sink in. "And now, fifteen years later, Al-Fassi is back and Aunt Miriam, two peregrine eyasses and one gyrfalcon are missing."

"There must have been a very good reason. Very good."

Rachel connected her laptop computer to the kitchen telephone line, clicked the Internet icon, and asked the driver to search for pete. The web hit on over a hundred thousand sites. She refined the search to add Raven.

"What are you doing?" Eric came to stand behind her.

"You asked why they would sell the falcons to a falconer. Here's your answer."

The PETE web page contained a mission statement, historical data about the organization, and claimed responsibility for a number of costly sabotage projects occurring within the past two years.

"PETE encourages members to do whatever is necessary to stop the advancement of Homo sapiens pillaging the environment."

"How does selling wild birds into slavery accomplish that?"

"It provides funding, say for an environmental counterattack, or for a political campaign of a candidate who would introduce legislation like the Nettleman Bill."

Eric pointed at the screen. "Why Raven?"

"That's the name I heard Igor use for the man who ordered them to retrieve the disk and watch me. I thought Johnson was Raven, but now I'm not convinced. There's a reference to

Raven somewhere in these logs."

She scanned the material, finally finding a citation under the heading news clippings, dated July 1984.

A People for the Ethical Treatment of the Earth (PETE) member known as Raven claimed credit on behalf of the organization for a series of devastating arson fires set at DDT manufacturing plants across the United States. Property damage is estimated to be in the millions. One man died.

Blah, blah, blah. Further down the page was another clipping.

Raven, code name for a member of the radical environmental group PETE (People for the Ethical Treatment of the Earth), is wanted for murder in connection with the death of a security guard at a DDT plant in eastern Nebraska. Raven claimed credit for the July blaze, saying PETE hoped to stop the distribution and use of the dangerous pesticide.

"So in other words, this Raven fellow is wanted for murder." Eric said.

"Right. And, as far as I know, the crime of murder doesn't have a statute of limitations. Which means Raven can still be tried and convicted."

Eric whistled. "That gives someone an incentive for murder."

Which explained why Raven had targeted her. She was leading the investigation into Aunt Miriam's disappearance. She and the others must be getting too close in their quest for information. The question was, how deeply was Aunt Miriam involved?

"Go back to the picture," Eric said. "Who do you think is taking it?"

"Mike Johnson, maybe?" Rachel tried wrapping her mind around the overload of information. "The way I see it, Forest masterminded the sale of the falcons to Sheikh Al-Fassi. The photographs substantiate his involvement. Now, fifteen years later, he's set up to do it again, and who shows up? Bursau. If word ever leaked out, Forest's political career would be over."

Eric sat down, propping one foot on the bench and resting his arm on his knee. "Where does Miriam fit into all of this?"

"I wish I knew." Was she guilty or in trouble? Rachel turned on the computer, typed Sheikh Al-Fassi in the search box, hit enter, then clicked on the first entry. "I suppose she could have been taking the photographs."

Eric scowled. "I doubt it. What are you looking for?"

"This." She turned the screen toward Eric. The web page documented the sheikh's commitment to the reintroduction of the peregrine falcon and preservation of the Houbara bustard. It gave details about an extensive research facility he had established near Riyadh that was used for propagation of the species. "The peregrine is an endangered species, right?"

"Technically, they've been delisted, but they're still protected by the Migratory Bird Treaty Act."

"Do all birders agree delisting is the right thing to do?"

"Of course not. In fact, a lot of us think we'll see a decline in the population now that they've lost their protection. Personally, I think it's too early to delist them."

All the pieces were there, and yet something didn't fit. The sheikh wanted birds. Miriam had birds. But even if Forest facilitated, why would Miriam sell the birds? She didn't need the money. Or did she? Hadn't she told Rachel that most of her assets were tied up in Bird Haven? Was she so land rich and cash poor that she would have stooped to participation in Forest's scheme?

Rachel's head, still aching from last night, was now clogged with new details. She studied the photographs again. In the background was a small cabin constructed of thin, notched, pine poles and nestled against the base of a large spruce tree. "Do you recognize this place?"

"Ja. It's a cabin that was used by the professors and students when they were gathering information on the peregrine populations in the park. It was off-limits to everyone but the professors and the graduate students."

Her pulse quickened. That narrowed things down. Only a certain number of people knew it was there. "Do you know how to get there?"

"Sure. We checked it out the other day."

"With the birdwatchers?"

Eric nodded, swinging his leg down from the bench. "It was empty."

"Did you go up there yourself?"

"No."

"Who went?"

Eric frowned. "Charles, Harry, and Forest."

Chapter 16

"If Aunt Miriam was hiding in the cabin and one of them knew it, he could have gone in while the others checked around the perimeter. Do you know how to get up there?"

"Ja, but I think we need to call Vic Garcia," Eric said. He rubbed his palms on his jeans and blotted his upper lip with the back of his hand. "We need Vic to send someone up there, and to pick up the others."

He was right. Charging up to the cabin without a plan was dangerous.

Rachel dialed the Sheriff's Department. The sheriff was out on a call.

"There's been an accident in the canyon," the woman on the desk said. "A cement mixer overturned, and it's blocking the road in both directions."

"This is an emergency," Rachel said. "I have to talk with him."

"I can try reaching him by radio. Hold, please." The desk clerk clicked off.

Rachel tapped her foot impatiently. After several minutes, the woman came back on the line. "He's not responding. I can have him call you when he comes in."

"But we need someone up here now," Rachel insisted, switching the phone to her other ear. Response time in New York City was better than this.

"Is this a life-threatening emergency?"

"Possibly"

"Is someone injured?"

"No."

"Then I have a deputy on duty, but unfortunately he's out on another call, too. I can send him up when he's finished if you like."

"Please do that." Rachel slammed down the phone, then shut down the computer and clicked the cover shut. "Igor said something about today being the day. I don't think we should wait."

"There's no way to know who or what we're dealing with out there. Look at what happened last night. Besides, it's all just speculation on our part."

"What if Aunt Miriam's in danger?"

"That's a chance we'll have to take. One or two hours isn't going to make the difference."

"It can."

They faced off. After several unsuccessful attempts at badgering Eric into divulging the cabin's location, Rachel scooped up her laptop and Miriam's spare set of car keys, and stormed out, leaving him to wait for Garcia's call. She knew trying to find the cabin with nothing more than a general sense of direction would be tantamount to finding a person in Manhattan using only psychic ability. Odds of about seven and a half million to one. And trekking alone into the wilderness was out of the question. Who else besides one of the men might know the cabin's location? Lark!

Banging in through the unlocked front door after only a cursory knock, Rachel found Lark cuddled in the easy chair, surrounded by Dorothy and Cecilia.

Lark glanced up. "You look a little teed off. Something the matter?"

"I think I know where Aunt Miriam is, but I can't get ahold of Garcia and Eric refuses to help me."

"What?" Dorothy said.

"Where?" Lark asked.

"I'll show you." Rachel recounted the events of the previous evening and her morning's conversation with Eric while she booted up the computer.

"We heard about the car," Dorothy said. "The fire chief told me he thought it was a rental, and that the Sheriff's Department was having trouble tracking the owner. What with all the tourists in town, it never occurred to me it was yours. Are you okay?"

"I'm a walking sprain."

Lark rearranged her foot on the ottoman. "Tell me about it."

Rachel brushed aside a twinge of guilt. "Lark and I found one of Bursau's computer disks," she explained, opening a photograph file. "This was on it. If you ask me, based on this picture, Forest is our man."

"I don't believe it," Dorothy protested. She turned to Lark. "Has she lost her mind?"

"No."

"What do you mean, no? We're talking about Forest Nettleman," cried Cecilia.

The bag of ice placed across Lark's ankle crashed to the floor as she leaned forward to study the photograph displayed on the laptop monitor. "Remember I told you about rumors of his arrest, Rachel? Well I talked to my father this morning. It seems Forest was an ecowarrior back in the sixties. Before it was fashionable."

"What, may I ask, is an ecowarrior?" Dorothy's face was a study in distaste.

"A person who believes in taking radical steps to protect the environment," explained Rachel.

"That sort of defines any of us," Cecilia said, uncrossing a pair of comely legs.

Lark stretched for her ice bag, repositioning her ankle on a pillow. "Apparently Forest got into environmental activism while he was a freshman at Northwestern University. He was arrested the first time in 1962 for chaining himself to an elm tree at a building site in Evanston, Illinois. He spent three days in jail and was sentenced to ninety days of community service."

"The first time?" echoed Dorothy.

Cecilia leaned toward her sister and whispered, "Oh, my, if he's a jailbird, he's certainly not suitable husband material."

"Cecilia!"

"Well…"

Dorothy shook her head in disbelief. "He seemed so normal. It doesn't seem possible that someone like Forest would get mixed up in something like this murder."

"It looks like he's in it up to his eyeballs," Cecilia said, flipping her fingers toward the picture of him with William and the sheikh.

"To really understand it, Dorothy, you have to know some

history of the environmental movement," explained Rachel. "I did some research, and discovered that most of the early conservation movement in the U.S. was through established organizations like the Sierra Club, the National Audubon Society, the Wilderness Society."

"Your basic mainstream America," Lark commented.

"Right. Then in 1970, the first Earth Day was held and the radicals came out of the woodwork. With the Vietnam war grinding to a halt, the protesters needed a new cause."

"The environment?" Dorothy asked.

Rachel nodded. "It was short-lived, though. By the mid-seventies the people wanting to work for conservation groups were career-oriented, degreed professionals."

"Like Forest," Cecilia said.

"Except, I bet some of them felt like the cause was lost," Lark added.

"Right again." Rachel stood and paced the length of the fireplace. "They formed a group called Earth First! in 1980. Disgruntled conservationists, they set out to be radical—in style, positions, philosophy, and organization."

"What did they do?" Dorothy leaned forward with rapt attention.

"Earth First!-ers spiked trees, sabotaged heavy equipment, cut fences. They placed an emphasis on strategic monkey-wrenching in defense of the wild."

Cecilia's mouth dropped open. "You're saying Forest was a gang member?"

"From the ground floor up." Rachel pivoted. "And based on what he said about the Nettleman Bill the other night, I'm beginning to think he went left when the groups fractured in the early nineties."

"Fractured in what way?" Dorothy asked.

"There was an internal push by some members of Earth First! to pacify and deradicalize the movement. Sort of the 'ecocrats' versus the 'ecoterrorists.' Anyway, the factions split, and the ecoterrorists formed new groups, blending with radical animal rights activists under banners like People for the Ethical Treatment of the Earth."

"PETE," Lark said.

"You've got it. Instead of lobbying for change in the conventional ways, these guys encourage members to take extreme actions in their fight for the Earth. Some groups even go so far as to advocate death to human beings. They have an 'end justifies the means' mentality."

Lark studied the computer screen. "You know, I wouldn't have believed it if I hadn't seen it."

"Oh, my, I hope they don't object to our using binoculars in the woods."

"Cecilia!" Dorothy gasped.

"Well…"

Rachel swept her hair into a ponytail, cupping her hands around the back of her head. "The question is, what do we do now?"

"These guys sound dangerous," Lark said. "I think we have to wait for Vic."

"And what if we're too late? Igor said something was going down today, and today is when Mike Johnson is showing the sheikh the birds. I think we need to hike up to the cabin and see if Aunt Miriam's there."

"Maybe she's there voluntarily," Cecilia suggested, twining and untwining her fingers in her lap.

"How can you say such a thing?" Dorothy said.

"It's okay. It's a possibility," Rachel said. Cecilia looked smug. Dorothy and Lark looked shocked. "Aunt Miriam could still be trying to protect Uncle William. Maybe in return for Forest's silence she was blackmailed into going along with his plan. Let's just say I'm not willing to sit around and wait to find out."

"Me neither," Cecilia said. "What do you want me to do?"

The other two women nodded that they were in, too. Rachel stared out the window, then turned to Lark. "Do you know where the cabin is?"

"Yeah, I can even show you. There's a trail map of the park in the right-hand top drawer of the desk in my office."

Rachel retrieved it and opened it in front of Lark.

"I'm not a hundred percent sure." She studied the map, her

braid swinging forward across her shoulder. "But, I think the best way is to go up to the Twin Owls trailhead. You'll find a jeep road that heads off at the junction of the two hiking trails. The day we went climbing, we veered right toward the Twin Owls formation. The other trail parallels Black Canyon Creek from a distance, and eventually joins the Cow Creek and Lawn Lake trails. The jeep road goes straight, and it doesn't look like it goes very far. But if you scoot behind the cabins, it goes back for quite a way. When you get to the end, you'll see a path heading off to the left."

Rachel tracked Lark's finger on the map. "Sort of ten o'clock from due north."

"Yeah. Get me a pen and I'll draw it for you." Lark etched a heavy line for the jeep trail, a lighter dashed line for the path, then marked the site of the cabin with a large X.

"How far back do you think it is?"

"Maybe nine miles altogether."

"You can't go traipsing up there by yourself," Cecilia said.

Four days ago, she might have agreed. In fact, four days ago the odds of getting her to brave the wilderness were nil to none. But things had changed. "Are you going with me?"

Cecilia straightened her shoulders. "Yes."

"Cecilia!"

"Oh, be quiet, Dorothy. Can't you see the girl's determined? And I can't say I blame her, either. If Miriam is up at that cabin, she may be in real trouble, and there's no telling when Vic or his deputy will show up."

"I don't think this is such a great idea," Dorothy said. "What if Mike Johnson arrives with the sheikh while you're attempting your rescue? You'll be outnumbered."

Rachel hated to point out that they could be outnumbered anyway.

"Wait, I have an idea." She picked up the phone, dialed Black Canyon Creek Ranch, and asked for Mike. Holding her hand over the mouthpiece, she whispered, "We're in luck. He's still there."

"What are you going to say to him?" Lark asked.

"I..." Rachel held up her hand. "Hello, Mike? Rachel

Stanhope. I just wanted to apologize for missing the tour of the mews last night." She flashed the women an 'okay' sign. "I was waylaid leaving the bar. Could I impose on you for another chance? Maybe this afternoon?" She waggled her head. "Of course, I understand. Another time, then." Rachel cradled the receiver, doubled her fists, and brought both elbows to her sides. "Yes."

"Is he giving you another tour?" Lark asked.

"Not today. He says he's scheduled to take Sheikh Al-Fassi small-game hunting in thirty minutes." For any chance of success, she and Cecilia needed more than that for a head start. But there was still time. "What the two of you are going to do is create a diversion designed to give Cecilia and me some extra time."

"You're kidding, right?" Lark said.

"Look, whatever is scheduled to happen, is happening today, in half an hour. If Mike Johnson and the sheikh are delayed, we buy ourselves that much extra time to get to Miriam."

"If she's at the cabin."

"Where else could she be, unless she's...?" Rachel let the question hang, refusing to give in to the thought. It was a plan born of desperation, but a plan nonetheless. "If we can just keep Johnson at the ranch, then Cecilia and I may be able to reach Miriam."

Lark sat up straighter. "So what kind of diversion are we talking?"

"Something that throws a monkey wrench into their plans," Dorothy said, getting into the swing of things.

Cecilia grinned. "Why not give them a dose of their own medicine?"

"Such as?" asked Rachel. There was nothing quite like a band of radical birdwatchers.

"How about disabling their cars?" Dorothy suggested.

"In broad daylight?" Lark tapped her cast. "Count me out."

"That is a problem," Cecilia clucked, then snapped her fingers. "I've got it. Potatoes! If you jam them tight inside an exhaust pipe, the car sputters and dies. It takes three or more days for the potato to shrink enough to be blown out. I doubt most people would ever figure it out."

It sounded like she'd done this before.

"Where did you learn that trick?" Lark asked.

Cecilia puffed herself up. "I've seen my share of radical days."

"It's that Jimmy Meyer's influence," Dorothy declared.

"Is not."

"Is too."

"Now that we've settled that," Lark interrupted, "I guess we should synchronize our watches and get this show on the road."

Rachel and Cecilia headed out after helping load Lark into Dorothy's car. They took the road to Bird Haven while Dorothy and Lark went to Safeway to buy a five-pound bag of potatoes.

Eric's truck was still parked in front of the Raptor House, and Rachel hoped he didn't spot them driving by in Miriam's car. She wondered if the sheriff had called, but knew she couldn't stop to find out. If she did, Eric would never let her leave.

The jeep road at the trailhead was barely visible. Two tracks of flattened grass wound into the forest from the far side of a small parking area. Tire tracks and small dirt clods indicated the road had been driven recently, but not by many.

Rachel steered Miriam's Land Cruiser onto the trail. "Hold on. Here we go." The vehicle jounced along the narrow road.

Trees crowded close on either side, branches scraping against the doors like fingernails dragging across a blackboard. Thin slivers of light filtered through the dense tree cover, casting lacy snowflake-patterned shadows on the ground and dashboard.

They hit a rock, and the springs in Rachel's seat squeaked. She bounced. The seat belt snapped tight across her sore shoulder, making her wince.

Cecilia fiddled with the map. "How far do you think we've come?"

"To the end of the road."

Rachel stopped and sized up the turnaround in front of her. It was a small area. Tire tracks matted the grass in tight circles, crushing the small white flowers growing like sprigs of rock candy in the thin soil. "We can't leave the car sitting out in the open. We'll have to find a place to hide it."

Cecilia pointed to a large boulder on the left. "We could try sneaking it in behind that big rock."

"Or we could try driving closer." Rachel pointed to an area that appeared to open to the west of the wall of trees.

Cecilia looked doubtful. "If it was possible to drive in, don't you think they would?"

"It's more private without a road. But the closer we can get to the cabin, the better." Rachel gunned the engine and headed down the line of trees, finding only one narrow opening. She maneuvered between the trunks of tall spruce, Douglas-fir, and ponderosa pine. Winding back and forth to parallel the footpath, she maintained the general direction of the X on the map. Finally, the trees grew thinner and closer together, and it became clear that they needed to find a place to park.

"We'll have to walk from here. At least the car's not noticeable from the clearing."

"Let's hope we can find it again," Cecilia pulled two medium-sized backpacks from the trunk. Each contained a flashlight, a water bottle, and a jacket. She handed one to Rachel and shouldered the other. "And that it's not dark before we get back."

Rachel added the cell phone to her backpack even though it didn't work in some places in the mountains. If they found Aunt Miriam and it worked from the cabin, Rachel would be thrilled.

They backtracked to the clearing and started up the small trail leading off in the direction Lark had marked on the map. The trees crowded together like pick-up sticks in a can. Sunlight struggled to reach the forest floor, and it grew colder.

After they'd hiked for half an hour, Rachel stopped. Was that a car she heard droning in the distance?

"Do you hear that, Cecilia?"

Cecilia's face looked ashen. "It sounds like an engine. Do you think we should turn around?"

"Not after we've come this far." Rachel calculated how much distance they had left to go. "We're almost there. Another half-hour, tops. A mile and a half."

"What if it's Forest, or Mike and the sheikh?"

Rachel pondered the question. "They don't know we're here,

so they're not going to skulk up the trail. They'll be talking. Business as usual. If they get too close, we'll slip into the trees, wait until they've passed, then follow them."

"How do you know they don't know we're here? Maybe Dorothy and Lark got caught."

Rachel felt a prickle of fear, then a flash of guilt for having put everyone in danger. "You're right, Cecilia. If you want to, I think you should go back. Just do me a favor, and stay out of sight so they don't know I'm up here."

Cecilia looked shocked. "I'm only asking sensible questions and pointing out the obvious. If you're not interested in facing the truth, then…"

"We don't have time to debate the issue, Cecilia. Either you're coming or you're not. Which is it?"

Cecilia sputtered like an angry chicken. "I'm coming."

Behind them the engine noise droned closer, the vibration splitting into two distinct sounds.

"I think there are two cars," Rachel said. "Come on, let's hurry." She pressed on up the path, her chest and lungs burning with the exertion. The altitude made her feel queasy and light-headed, and pulling deep breaths made her cough. Cecilia kept pace, and wasn't even winded.

"Rachel, is that the cabin?" Cecilia pointed in the direction of a small juniper tree. The sharp peak of a roof stuck up.

Adrenalin pumped into Rachel's veins. Her heart raced. A man's voice in the distance gave her another jolt, and she swung the backpack off her shoulder and dug for her phone. The sun dropped toward Long's Peak, throwing afternoon shadows across the tops of the trees. At best, they had another hour of daylight.

"Take this." She pressed the cell phone into Cecilia's hand. "Stay here! If I'm not back by the time those guys draw close, slip back in the woods and try calling for help. Walk around until you find a spot where you can get a signal."

Cecilia planted her hands on her hips. "You're not leaving me behind."

"Shhhh!" Rachel drew another deep breath and exhaled. "Look, we don't know who's up there, or who's behind us. It only makes sense that we serve as each other's backup. If I'm not back by the time those men get here, let them pass and try calling for help. Then double back to the car. If I'm not back within an hour, get out of here. Do you understand?"

Cecilia nodded.

Rachel hugged her, started toward the cabin, then turned around. "Cecilia?"

"Yes?"

"Be careful."

Chapter 17

The cabin sat in the middle of a clearing. A wide, squat, log building with a multitude of screened windows. From any direction Rachel approached, she could be seen.

Damn!

She listened for sounds of the men on the trail, then for sounds from the cabin. A raptor screeched, but she couldn't be sure if it was from inside or from the cliffs that reached toward the sky behind the cabin. A bee buzzed, gathering pollen from a cluster of yellow wildflowers. The meadow grasses crackled with heat while a cold chill pulsed from the woods behind her.

The best approach seemed to be from the rear of the cabin. The front had a wide, roofed porch, and the side walls could be seen from the footpath.

Rachel hugged the trees and circled around back. There was a door with two small windows flanking it. A set of rickety steps led to a small, square deck.

Here goes!

She crouched low to the ground, the way she'd seen SWAT team members do on TV when they approached a hostage situation. But somehow they were quieter. With every step she nailed a twig, jumping as it snapped, sure any second her position would be detected.

Nothing happened. No sounds from the cabin. No sounds from the men on the path. She hoped Cecilia was okay.

When she reached the back wall, she pressed herself flat against the logs. The windows were high, even for someone her height. She needed something to stand on. An old stump stuck out of the ground too far away to be of use, and it was the only thing in sight.

She tried scaling the logs, jamming the toes of her shoes and her fingers into the cracks, and pulling herself up. Every time she gained, a piece of bark flaked off the logs and she slipped back to the ground.

The back door had a window.

Gathering her courage, she crept up the steps. The second one creaked loudly.

Rachel froze.

She held her breath, counted to ten, then continued up the steps. Slowly she eased her foot off the offending board and stepped to the next higher one.

The small deck had two broken boards, forcing Rachel to lean sideways to peer through the window.

The cabin was larger than she'd realized. The back door opened into a kitchen with bright yellow curtains and a metal table with four folding chairs. There was a counter set up with a small propane cookstove, and a sink with a pump. A room off the kitchen appeared to be a bathroom. Rachel guessed it was more of an attached latrine.

She could see part of the main room. There were some homemade log chairs, a rocking chair, another table, and a staircase to the second floor. That had to be where the sleeping rooms were.

The cabin appeared empty. Where was Miriam? Had she been wrong?

Suddenly Miriam appeared in front of the door. Rachel gasped, stepped backward, and nearly fell through the deck. The boards splintered and cracked beneath her weight. The railing flopped as she tried to steady herself.

"Rae! What are you doing here?" Miriam propped open the back door and offered Rachel a hand. "How did you find me?"

"Eric and I figured it out." Rachel grabbed her aunt's arm. "We have to get out of here. I'll explain everything once we're back at the car."

"What are you babbling about, dear? We can't leave now."

"Aunt Miriam, I don't know why you're up here, but we have to go. Trust me, please!"

"I'm not going anywhere." Miriam straightened her small frame and walked into the front room. Three birdcages sat on the floor near the fireplace. In Rachel's guesstimation each one measured two feet by two feet by two feet. There was no way they could lug these cages out by themselves, much less escape detection.

The gyrfalcon spread his wings until the ends caught at the mesh. The baby peregrines hissed and spit.

She knew better than to argue with Miriam. Her aunt was strong-willed and stubborn, traits shared by most of the Wilder women. Arguing might make her tether herself to the bird cages, and they'd lose precious time. Rachel tried another tack.

"Look, you're the prime suspect in the murder of Donald Bursau, and Sheriff Garcia thinks you've run away to avoid arrest. Or to sell the birds."

"Nonsense. I'm here to protect them."

"From whom? Forest?"

Miriam's head drooped. "Fifteen years ago, your Uncle William and Forest got caught up in some scheme to raise money for an underground environmental movement. It was a radical notion for radical times. The peregrines were dying because of DDT use in South and Central America. It was a mass extermination of a wonderful species."

"Whose idea was it? Forest's?"

"No. They were approached by a spokesperson for the Environmentalists for Earth movement."

The group that spawned PETE. "Did Uncle William and Forest know each other back then?"

"Not well, but we lived in the same area. Forest was running for public office on the environmental ticket, and he knew of your Uncle William's research through connections with one of the university regents. And through Charles."

"Charles? I didn't know he knew Forest."

"Oh, they were old friends, from back in the sixties, until they had some sort of falling out."

The sixties. That's when Forest had first been arrested for environmental activism.

"Do you know how they knew each other?"

"No, but Charles warned William to steer clear of any of Forest's schemes. William wouldn't listen."

"Did he say why?"

"Just that any plan involving Forest was too risky to get involved with. William should have listened."

Something didn't add up, but there wasn't any time to analyze the situation. Rachel stepped to the window and parted the curtains, peering toward the footpath. There was still no sign of anyone approaching, but it wouldn't be long before the men who were following arrived. "Aunt Miriam, could we finish this discussion on the way back to the car?"

"I'm not leaving without the birds."

"We can come back for them with Sheriff Garcia."

Miriam planted herself in the rocking chair. "I'm not leaving without them."

Rachel needed to convince her she was in danger. But how?

"Do you want to hear the rest of the story or not, dear?" Miriam sighed. She didn't wait for Rachel's reply. "Charles worked with William then, and they had a terrible argument. The plan was for William to note in the records that the eyasses died, and that he disposed of the bodies. Then he was to bring the birds here to meet with some Arab sheikh known for his interest in falconry. The sheikh was going to take the birds back to Saudi Arabia, hunt with them one year, then release them."

"Sheikh Al-Fassi."

"That might have been his name. I don't actually remember."

"So what happened?"

"William carried out his part, and met Forest and the sheikh with the birds. Toward the end of the transaction, someone spirited the briefcase of money off the table in the kitchen and disappeared with it."

"A member of the Environmentalists for Earth?"

"Most likely. After that there were some bombings of DDT factories, and then that poor security guard died." Miriam twisted her hands in her lap. "There were pictures taken of the transaction."

"The ones Bursau acquired."

"Environmentalists for Earth delivered a copy to William of the one with Forest, the sheikh, and himself. I didn't realize there were others until Bursau showed up, claiming to have copies of more."

"How did he get them?"

"He said he received them anonymously. I suppose we'll never know for sure, dear."

"From the same person who was blackmailing Uncle William?"

"Most likely. Early on, we were asked for money. And we paid. William could have been charged as an accessory to murder, or worse. The government considered the bombings acts of terrorism. Eventually the group disbanded. The more radical members formed a group called the People for the Ethical Treatment of the Earth."

"PETE."

Miriam nodded. "After that, the calls stopped. We thought it was over."

Something was out of whack. "What part did Mike Johnson play in all of this?"

"None. He wasn't involved at all."

Rachel frowned. "Then who shot the photographs? Did Forest know they were being taken?"

"He claims he didn't. He claims he was being blackmailed, just like us. Bursau had contacted him, too. The reporter intended to expose everything, including the upcoming deal."

"What upcoming deal?"

"That's what I asked when Charles told me. It seems Forest was planning to sell the eyasses and gyrfalcon to the sheikh, to get more capital to fund his upcoming campaign." Miriam kicked the rocker into motion. "I didn't want to believe it at first. Forest and William had made a pact never to involve themselves in anything subversive ever again, and over the years had worked together, using more mainstream methods to further the environmental cause. I truly believed that Forest had switched to fighting from the inside out, and was dedicated to changing the system with long-term effects. The Nettleman Bill is a perfect example. I never once doubted him. Until now."

"What made you change your mind?"

"Charles discovered some sheikh was scheduled to be here this week. He's registered at the Black Canyon Creek Lodge."

Charles. His name kept cropping up. "Did you tell Charles about the photographs Bursau had?"

"Of course, dear. He and I are old friends, after all. But he already knew."

Rachel recalled Charles's words. "Miriam and I have decided to live together." Pictured his fingers worrying the signet ring he wore on his right hand. The finger. The missing fingertip!

In the last photograph she'd seen, the person opening the briefcase had his face obscured, yet something in that picture had struck her as oddly familiar. She bet if they enlarged the photograph and looked closely at the hands, they would see a missing fingertip. Charles was the man in the picture! She'd pegged the wrong man! Charles was Raven.

"Aunt Miriam, we have to get out of here."

"I told you, I'm not leaving without the birds."

"But don't you see? Charles is behind all of this. He's the PETE member, not Forest."

"Nonsense, dear." Miriam rocked the chair harder, making it creak. The birds screeched.

Rachel described the picture of Charles holding the briefcase. "He thought he was safe, Aunt Miriam. He'd fooled all of you for years. He knew he was in trouble, though, when Bursau started asking questions and you told him about the copies of the photographs. Seeing his hands is all it would have taken for you to piece the puzzle together."

Miriam's face lost all color. Her fingers gripped the arms of the chair.

"Aunt Miriam, did Charles ask you to marry him?"

Miriam's head snapped up. "Yes. But I said no. He and I are friends, that's all. I don't think of him in that way."

"He told us you agreed to live with him. Sort of a 'trial marriage.'"

"That's absurd. I agreed to no such thing."

"It's because, as his wife, you couldn't be forced to testify against him." Rachel wondered if Colorado recognized common-law marriage. "The point is—"

"Your niece is too damn smart for her own good."

Rachel turned. Charles stood in the doorway between the front room and the kitchen, pointing a gun in her direction.

"Then what she's telling me is true." Miriam half-rose from the chair.

"Sit down, Miriam." He strode into the room, a vision in

camouflage. His pants and jacket were three shades of green blobs mixed with brown blobs. If Rachel hadn't known better, she would say he was fresh out of boot camp. The diamond glittered from his earlobe. Light glinted off the steel shaft of the revolver. "I was hoping we could avoid this."

Rachel hadn't seen anyone follow him in, and there didn't appear to be anyone out front. Had Charles come alone? She'd heard two vehicles on the road.

"Your friends from the cliff are out there," he said. "So don't go getting any bright ideas."

"Why are you doing this, Charles?" Miriam reached out and touched his sleeve. He jerked his arm away.

"For Earth. There's no more time for negotiation. It's time to take back the land for the sake of survival. The land was meant to breathe. Without breath it can't sustain life."

Rachel sidled closer to Miriam while Charles pontificated, one arm stretched across the mantel. The gun barrel bobbed in time with the cadence of his voice. He didn't seem to notice her movement, so absorbed was he in his own voice and message.

"It's time to tear up the asphalt and allow the roads to rehabilitate to their natural state. It's time to blow up the dams and let the water flow free. It's time to tear down the cities, and allow the land to revert to its primeval state. Humans need to become animals again. Animals need to roam free."

"Let me get this straight," Rachel said. "You take an anti-society, anti-progress stance, and yet you drive a brand new SUV, wear a diamond stud in your ear, and aspire to live at Bird Haven."

"Shut up."

"Charles!"

"She's screwed up the plan, Miriam." His voice sounded gruff, apologetic. "She's screwed up everything."

"Exactly what was the plan, Charles?" asked Rachel. She could see Igor out the window now. He sat on the top step of the porch, leaning against one of the columns that held up the roof. "Were you planning to sell the birds for money to fund more of PETE's activities, or just send them home with Miriam once you'd framed Forest and Mike Johnson for bird trafficking and murder?"

"You really are clever." He smiled, but the forced warmth never reached his cold, blue eyes. "The birds were never for sale, but Bursau had guessed it was me in the photographs."

Rachel thought back to his comments on the Nettleman Bill. She had construed them as negative, when in fact he'd been advocating a harsher reaction to Mike Johnson's encroachment on Rocky Mountain National Park and Aunt Miriam's land. She heard his words in her head. "The only thing that'll stop him is someone hitting him hard in the pocketbook, like Miriam shutting down access so he's forced to find an alternate route."

From what she'd read about PETE activists, they believed in zeroing in on the most vulnerable point of a wilderness-destroying project. In this case, access. Without Miriam's permission to cross Bird Haven land, Mike Johnson would lack the access he needed to obtain the BLM land permit.

"Figure it out?" he asked.

Rachel shrugged, resting her hand on Aunt Miriam's shoulder. "I figure you set up a meeting with Donald Bursau to purchase the disks. His mistake was trusting you, which is why he erased all traces of the photographs off his hard drive."

"He planned on trading the disks for cash. Too bad I couldn't take the risk of him talking."

"So you killed him. Did you do the same to the person who took the original photographs?"

"The dirtbag was only supposed take photographs of Forest and William."

"Instead, he shot pictures of you, too. Was he blackmailing you as well?"

"What do you think?" Charles tapped the butt of the gun against the mantel. "I couldn't afford to keep paying him. Who would have guessed that copies of the photos would end up at Birds of a Feather magazine? Apparently the dirtbag's kid was moving, found them in a box in his garage, and called Bursau. He paid the guy a hundred bucks. That's all. Just a hundred bucks for those photos."

Rachel felt Miriam tense, and she squeezed her aunt's shoulder. "What are you going to do with us?"

Charles straightened up. "I liked my original idea." he said, waggling the gun, " But you must realize that the plan has changed."

Chapter 18

Strategically Charles's new plan was brilliant, and he didn't resist the opportunity to brag. He and his goons had found Cecilia on the road and, convinced they'd been sent to help by Lark or one of the others, she'd told them everything. Charles assured her the sheriff had taken Forest into custody, and that Dorothy, Lark, and Eric were being held for questioning at Black Canyon Creek Ranch.

"Where is Cecilia now?" Rachel demanded.

"She and your cell phone are being held back at the truck."

"And what, may I ask, were your plans for me?" Miriam asked, her voice quavering.

"I was hoping you and I could work something out," he said, running a finger down the side of her face. "But I guess not, huh?" A tear slipped down beside her nose, and he turned away. "The park is big. And it's so darned easy to get disoriented when you're hiking in the backcountry. You know, even in June, people die from hypothermia when they're not wearing proper clothing."

Rachel swallowed. The sun was dropping, and the chill in the room attested to the truth in his statement. She considered trying to take Charles out with what she'd learned in self-defense class, but even if she succeeded, there were two more outside to contend with. She could never take Igor. And then there was the gun to consider.

No, she had to buy them more time, and hope that Cecilia had been able to use the cell phone before she'd been caught. "What about the photographs?"

"What about them? I destroyed all the disks."

"Except the one I have. It contains pictures of you stealing the briefcase."

Charles moved toward her, his eyes unreadable in the dim light. "You've seen that photograph?"

"Better. I have a copy of it."

"Where?" His hand clamped around her arm, and Rachel

winced.

"At Bird Haven."

He let go of her arm and cursed. "Lark told me you got only documents off that disk."

Lark? That's right, he'd visited her the day after the accident on Lumpy Ridge. She must have told him about finding the disk and retrieving the files. Rachel remembered telling her the photos couldn't be accessed. "No wonder you thought you were safe."

Charles backhanded her, then jerked open the front door. "Larry, get in here."

Igor stepped into the room. "What's up?"

"We have a problem. I need you to keep an eye on Miriam." Charles grabbed a high-powered flashlight. "I'll be back in an hour."

Rachel flashed a reassuring smile in her aunt's direction before Charles dragged her out the door. He shoved her roughly down the steps. She fell, tearing the knee out of her pants and reopening the puncture cuts on her leg caused by the cactus spines. "Ouch."

"Shut up." He jammed the gun in her back, and pushed her ahead of him down the path.

Night locked in the forest. She heard the occasional rustle of a nocturnal creature, and for the first time actually wished for a mountain lion. Any distraction would be welcome.

Branches tore at her clothes. Her boot slipped up and down, raising a blister on her heel. "Can we rest for a minute?"

"No." He shoved her, his hand square in the middle of her back, knocking the wind from her lungs. She coughed and stumbled. He shoved her again.

"How many copies of the picture did you make?"

"Why?"

"Don't toy with me," he said, his breath hot against her neck. "Who besides Miriam did you tell about the pictures? Have you shown them to anyone else?"

"No," she lied.

At the truck, he opened the rear passenger-side door, checked to see that the child protection latch had been flipped, then shoved her down onto the backseat. Cecilia lay curled on the floor. Duct tape sealed her mouth, and her hands were bound behind her back.

"Are you okay?"

Cecilia nodded.

"Did you make—"

"Shut up!"

Cecilia shook her head. Now that she knew help was not an option, Rachel's mind raced, skimming over ways to escape. She considered choking him while he drove, but that would only result in another car accident. Better to take her chances at Bird Haven.

She could see him in the rearview mirror. He glanced up every so often, but he shared his attention with the road. That might make it possible for her to free Cecilia's hands. Rachel pulled at the tape binding Cecilia's hands.

Cecilia gasped.

"What are you doing back there? Sit up."

Rachel leaned back against the seat.

The truck jounced over ruts and tree branches as Charles sped down the road toward Bird Haven. Rachel managed to bend down again, and pull the car keys from Cecilia's pocket. Stretching with her arm, she kept her face centered in the rearview mirror and sawed at the tape. It snagged, frayed, then finally snapped in two. Rachel signaled to Cecilia to lie still, then whispered a silent prayer that Eric would be there when they reached the house.

Both Bird Haven and the Raptor House lay dark. So much for a God. Charles killed the lights and coasted to a stop near the front door. Jumping out, he yanked open the rear door. "Get out."

Rachel slipped the keys into Cecilia's cupped hands and pushed herself across the seat, blocking his view of the older woman. "Can't we talk about this, Charles? I know you don't like me, but I can't believe you really want to hurt Aunt Miriam or Cecilia."

"I'll do what I have to for the cause."

"Spoken like a true fanatic."

"Get the picture." He jerked her away from the truck, slammed the door, and pushed her up the front steps.

"I don't have the keys," she said. "I left them back in my car." She hoped he wouldn't realize Cecilia had them, hoped he believed her lie.

Charles produced his own set. "Not to worry. Miriam trusts me."

"Her mistake." Now her only chance lay in getting away before Charles got his hands on the photographs, which meant she'd have to make a break for it soon. Aunt Miriam would be safe if Rachel was at large. She'd become a bargaining chip.

Rachel needed a way to distract Charles.

The lock tumbler clicked.

Perky! Day or night, the parakeet never failed to dive-bomb her as she entered the house. Let's hope he's enough of a distraction. She readied herself to run. Charles had left the truck keys in the ignition. If she could get back outside and into the truck, she could go for help.

Rachel reached for the light switch, but Charles clubbed her hand away with the butt of his gun. "No lights."

He produced a flashlight from his pocket. The beam flickered across her tennis racket, still leaning against the wall. A weapon! Now all she needed was Perky. Where the heck was he when you wanted him?

"Which room?"

"The study."

"Move it." He prodded her in the side with the barrel of the gun. She guided herself along the wall. Edging closer and closer to the tennis racket, she waited for Perky to attack. Had something happened to him?

At the last possible moment, Rachel saw the flash of white. Charles raised his arms and batted at the bird. "What the..."

Rachel groped for the tennis racket. Her hand found the grip in the dark. She swung, clipping the side of Charles's head.

"Why, you little..." He whirled and fired. She felt a sharp pain, then realized Perky had plucked out some of her hair. Rachel swung the racket again. This time the frame connected with Charles's head. He cursed, and fired again. "You'll pay for this!"

He wrenched the racket from her grip and leaned heavily against the door. She turned, stumbled in the dark, and dashed toward the living room. Ducking into the hallway, she slid into the shadow of the sitting room doorway and froze. She heard him bump against a wall.

"Where'd you go?" She heard him stop at the junction of the two hallways. "Straight or right, Perky?"

Straight, straight.

Perky whizzed past her head.

Traitor!

"When I find you, you're going to die." He moved past the doorway. Hadn't he seen the bird? She waited. It sounded like he had stopped again. Maybe he was waiting for her to give away her hiding place.

She held her ground. Finally he moved past, his footsteps clattering on the stone floor of the bar.

Rachel pressed herself flat against the wall, drew two deep breaths, then backtracked down the hall toward the entrance.

"There you are." He pounded up behind her, and she sprinted toward the door. Only six more feet. The tennis racket lay on the floor, and she kicked it toward him.

"Ow!"

Good, she must have caught his shin. She wrenched open the front door, slamming it shut behind her and bounding down the stairs to the truck. Sliding onto the driver's seat, she yanked the door shut and threw the locks.

The keys. Where were the keys? They no longer dangled from the ignition.

"Looking for these?"

Rachel jumped at the sound of Cecilia's voice in the back seat. The woman sat up, clanking the keys together like wind chimes on a breezy day.

"You scared me." Rachel snatched the keys, testing each in the ignition until one fit.

Charles's fist slammed into the glass beside her face, causing it to fracture into splinters. He drew a bead on the window with the gun. Rachel stared. Her heart hammered. Then she cranked the starter and threw the truck into reverse. A shot ricocheted off the hood of the cab as she peeled out of the driveway. Charles chased them on foot for a short way, then limped to a stop.

"Try the phone, Cecilia."

The cell phone connection was bad, but Cecilia managed to convince the dispatcher it was an emergency.

"The sheriff's out on a call," Cecilia said. "He's up at Black Canyon Creek Ranch."

"Great." Rachel made a hard left onto the ranch road and sped past the burned-out hulk of her rental car. Fishtailing up the road, she caught air off the washboard. Whipping into the parking lot, she laid on the horn. The sheriff and Mike Johnson were on the porch, talking with Dorothy and Lark.

"Hey, what's with all the commotion?" Johnson demanded, when Rachel jumped out of the truck. "I have dinner guests inside who—"

"Charles Pendergast is the man you're looking for, Sheriff. He just tried to kill me. He's holding Aunt Miriam in a cabin in the park. He's headed back up there now."

"Whoa, slow down there." Sheriff Garcia ambled over. "That's a mighty big accusation."

"It's true, Vic." Cecilia rose from the back seat. "He tied me up."

"What? Are you okay?" Dorothy charged down the steps and yanked open the passenger-side door, helping Cecilia to the ground.

Garcia stroked his mustache. "Mike caught these two ladies jamming potatoes into the exhaust pipes of the cars in his parking lot. They tell me it was your idea, Rachel. Some crazy notion that Mike and the sheikh were headed out to do some trafficking in wild birds."

"We thought Forest had arranged it. I don't know where he is, but—"

"He's inside, talking with my deputy."

"We were wrong, Sheriff. It wasn't Forest." Rachel rubbed her temples. "I mean, he was involved in the original sale, the one Bursau was planning to write about. But he wasn't involved in Aunt Miriam's disappearance."

"You say Charles kidnapped her?"

"Not exactly." Rachel tried to stay calm. Time was wasting. "Charles convinced her that she had to get the birds away and out of danger."

"I told you," Lark said.

"But now that he didn't get the picture—"

"What picture?" Garcia asked.

"The one on the disk that Lark and I recovered the day we went climbing up on Twin Owl. There were actually three."

"Why didn't you tell me?"

"Because you would have confiscated the disk, and I wanted to see what was on it."

"Where's the disk now?"

"Udall has it." She told him about the deal she'd struck. "But I copied the files onto a disk that's in my laptop computer in Aunt Miriam's car. It's up near the cabin."

"What do the pictures show?" Johnson asked.

"Forest, my uncle William and Sheikh Al-Fassi exchanging birds for money. And one shows the hands of the man who took the money that turned up missing, hands belonging to Charles Pendergast. He hired someone to take pictures of the exchange so he could blackmail Forest and Uncle William. Ironic, isn't it? He was caught by his own snare."

Sheriff Garcia bounded down the steps two at a time, then broke into a run toward his patrol car. "Mike, call dispatch and have them send some backup. Rachel, you come with me. You're going to have to show me where to go."

Jumping in the cruiser, she directed him back past Bird Haven and up the jeep road. They saw no sign of Charles, but Rachel knew he was in the woods somewhere. "I hope your backup gets here fast."

"Why didn't you call me right away?"

"Eric and I tried. He stayed at Bird Haven, waiting for your call. I stormed out and went to Lark's."

Garcia steered through a deep rut. The oil pan on the patrol car scraped. "Do you know where Eric is now?"

"No." Her mind raced through the possibilities. He might

have gone looking for Forest, Charles, Harry, or the sheriff. Or he might have grown tired of waiting and headed up to the cabin alone. She hadn't seen him when she'd come down with Charles.

"Okay, this is as far as I can go in this thing," Garcia said, wheeling the patrol car into the clearing. "Where's Miriam's car?"

"A little way farther, but Cecilia has the keys. Or they're in the back of Charles's truck somewhere."

"This is what you're going to do," Garcia said. "You're going to stay put until the backup arrives. Do you hear me?"

"I can't." She nearly hyperventilated at the thought of Charles trekking up from below and her sitting in the patrol car like bait. "Charles is back there. I know it."

Garcia narrowed his eyes. "You're probably right. Maybe you're safer with me. Let's go, but you stay behind me and out of trouble."

They followed the beam of his flashlight along the path to the cabin. When they drew within fifty yards, Garcia switched off the light and signaled her to follow him. He drew his gun from his holster, pointing with it to the back steps. "I'm going to go in through here. You keep your eyes open. Hoot like an owl if you see anyone—anyone—approaching. You understand?"

Rachel nodded.

The sheriff crept to the back door, and Rachel hunkered down in the grass, jumping at every crack and pop, keeping her eyes open. Garcia eased open the screen door and slid inside. There came a sound from behind Rachel. She whirled around.

"Hoo, hoo," she uttered, then a hand clamped over her mouth.

"Boo." Charles kneed her in the back, forcing her to stand, then pointed his gun at her head. "What do you say we go join the party?"

Rachel kicked at the grass as he pushed her forward, forcing her up the stairs. Suddenly there was a streak of movement from their right, and someone sideswiped them, knocking them both to the ground. Rachel rolled away and scrambled to her feet.

Spotlighted in the light from the window, Eric perched astride Charles, roping his hands behind his back. Harry leaned against the railing, dangling the gun from his index finger. "Ride 'em, cowboy."

Once Charles was secured, the three of them sidled in the back door, prepared to help Sheriff Garcia. No help was necessary. Frankenstein had offered him no resistance, and Igor had been asleep in the chair.

Two hours from the time Rachel bashed Charles with the tennis racket, Miriam and the birds were home. The sheriff had taken Charles, his accomplices, Forest, and Rachel's computer into custody. Rachel wondered if she'd ever see it again. Mike Johnson had dropped the charges against Dorothy and Lark, and the birdwatchers had gathered at Bird Haven. All except for the Hendersons and Gertie, whom no one had called. Kirk Udall had shown up on his own.

"What do you think will happen to Forest?" Dorothy asked, settling onto the sofa in the family room.

"It's hard to say," Eric said. "He wasn't the one who set the fires at the DDT plants, and he didn't specifically fund any of those fires, so I doubt they can charge him with murder. And the statute of limitations on illegal bird trafficking is seven years."

"Yeah, but by the time I'm through with my story, I doubt he'll ever be reelected," Udall said.

"Why go for the throat?" Lark asked. "Why not write about the good things Forest's done for the environment?"

"Yes, why not?" Dorothy chimed in. "Or maybe you could write about Mike Johnson's plans to sell Sheikh Al-Fassi American birds to help the repopulation of the peregrine in Saudi Arabia."

"That's not the story he wants to tell." Rachel slumped into her chair. "The story the magazine wants is about the men who committed the crimes, and their motives for doing so."

"What do you think William's motive was?" Miriam asked.

Rachel glanced up, surprised to see her aunt. Miriam took a seat near the patio door, lacing her fingers in her lap.

"I think he believed in a cause," Rachel answered. "I think Uncle William and Forest were convinced that the cost of selling the peregrines was worth the price if it meant funding to help stop the widespread use of DDT. They were merely misguided men."

"And Charles?"

"He's crazy. He believes in his cause—a total subversion of the system. A cause worthy of murder and mayhem. The men are not so unalike."

"How can you compare them?" Cecilia protested. "Charles almost killed us."

"I'm not saying they're the same type of men. I'm just saying they all believed that what they were doing was right. They all believed that the end justified the means. Charles just took it one step further. He believed the end was justified, no matter what."

"Is that how you think, Kirk?" Miriam asked.

The reporter colored. "What are you getting at? Is this where you ask me to omit telling William's part in this story?"

"No." Miriam shook her head sadly. "I guess I'm asking you to consider the cause."

"Look at all of the good things they've done," Rachel urged. "Think of the good Forest could continue to do, given the right support."

Udall eyed Rachel. "I'll tell you what. I'll think about it."

"That's all I'm asking."

"So, are you going to be around on Saturday, Mr. Udall?" Cecilia asked.

"I'm not sure. Why?"

"Because we hold our EPOCH birdwatching expeditions on Saturday. If you're still around, be here by eight o'clock sharp."

"I just might come by."

Cecilia winked at Rachel. Dorothy nudged her in the ribs. "You better watch out, or Cecilia's going to start trying to fix you up, too."

Perky chose that moment to swoop into the room and perch on a painting above Miriam's head.

"About time you showed up," Rachel said. "You need some training."

You got a problem, Chicky Baby?

"No, but you need to work on your timing."
Perky fluffed his feathers. Stuff it.

Common Raven

Corvus corax
Family: Corvidae (includes jays, crows, and ravens)

appearance: A large, glossy black bird with long, rounded wings and a wedge-shaped tail, the raven ranges from twenty-two to twenty-six inches in length. Larger than a crow, it is distinguished by a thick bill and shaggy throat feathers.

range: In North America, the raven breeds from northwestern Alaska, the Canadian Arctic, and Greenland south to Maine, northern Georgia, northern Michigan, North Dakota, and through the western United States and Mexico to Nicaragua. It winters in most of its breeding range. Throughout their range, ravens are usually seen scavenging alone or in pairs.

habitat: Ravens tend to live in wooded areas, often mountainous or hilly, and do not wander far from where they were raised. Nests are built in trees or on cliffsides. Food is temporarily cached at nearby sites, often buried.

call: The largest songbird, its cry varies widely—from a raspy raa-aa or aack to a raucous croak to a low, guttural krock to a clear, bell-like tone.

behavior: Ravens hop two or three times to get airborne, but once in flight they are amazing acrobats and will soar, dive, tumble, and roll. Opportunistic feeders, they take advantage of any potential food source, from garbage dumps to carrion. In fact, they seem to possess uncanny powers, not only to detect food but also to pass the word to others of their kind. Creative problem-solvers in the pursuit of food, they have been known to untie knots and unzip zippers, and to make off with car keys and other shiny objects.

relationship to man: The raven has played an important role in various cultures, mythologies, and writings. In Norse mythology, the god Odin had two ravens fly the world each day to keep him informed of what was happening. Viking warriors used the raven as their emblem when they invaded Europe. And the Plains Indians considered the raven an important spirit animal, an omen of good luck and bearer of news. Disparaged in Western literature, the raven was persecuted for damage to crops, game birds, and sickly farm animals. Baited, trapped, and shot, the ravens numbers decreased until corvids were added to the Migratory Bird Treaty in 1972. Now a federally protected species, the common raven is again becoming common.

Acknowledgments

Like every author, I owe a great deal to the people who supported, encouraged, and believed in me along the way. I wish to express my gratitude to members of the Rocky Mountain Fiction Writers, who helped critique this manuscript and taught me my craft. There are too many of you to name individually, but you know who you are. A special thanks to Janet Grill, a sister of my heart who was always there to "give me the speech."

My gratitude goes to everyone who supplied me with technical information, including Dick Coe and Joan Childers, rangers at Rocky Mountain National Park; Susan Ward, president of Estes Park Bird Club; Alice Gray; Michael Lee Stills, volunteer services coordinator of the Jeffco Open Space; Dan Williams and Bryan Posthumus, Raptor Project personnel; COBirders online, especially Ronda Woodward; Kern Karkos of the Denver Public Library; John Turner of the Denver Zoo bird staff; Sandy Cleva of the U.S. Fish and Wildlife Service; Dave Dixon of Aurora Raptors in Utah; and Kathy Konishi, Dave Croonquist, and Jerry Craig of the Colorado Division of Wildlife, for sharing their invaluable expertise.

A special thanks to my agent, Peter Rubie; to Alice Orr; Barry Neville, Harry McKinlay, and Georgeanne Nelson and to Cindy Hwang, who used her pen judiciously.

Last, I need to thank my children: Mardee, Danielle, Addie, Mike, Gin, and Cherie, for all they put up with over the years; and my husband, Wes Goff, who always believed in me. Thank you for making this possible.

Printed in Great Britain
by Amazon